HIS
ONLY
SON
OUR
LORD

A TOWER
BOOK

HIS ONLY SON OUR LORD

IDEAS ABOUT THE CHRIST

KENT S. KNUTSON

AUGSBURG PUBLISHING HOUSE
MINNEAPOLIS, MINNESOTA

HIS ONLY SON, OUR LORD

Scripture quotations are from the Revised Standard Version of the Bible, copyright 1946 and 1952 by the Division of Christian Education of the National Council of Churches.

Hymns from the *Service Book and Hymnal* (SBH) are used by permission of the Commission on the Liturgy and Hymnal.

Manufactured in the United States of America

Preface

"Therefore let us leave the elementary doctrines of Christ and go on to maturity. . . . And this we will do if God permits" (Heb. 6:1-3).

This book is intended for people who want solid food rather than milk. The aim is to discuss some of the ideas about the Christ that are not touched upon in the more regular teaching programs in the congregation and to do so in a way that would be of interest to someone not trained in technical theology. Every Christian, of course, is a theologian. Theology is reflection upon the nature and content of the faith, and everyone who calls himself Christian (and perhaps some who do not) is involved in this pursuit.

Not every question is raised or answered. Nor is there an attempt to document each idea. A study in ideas is somewhat different from a Bible study or a scientific treatise. Here each man's opinion is valuable, although the final judgment must be left to a solid interpretation of the Scriptures.

Take and read. And joy to you!

Contents

Contents

I Believe...

And in Jesus Christ
HIS ONLY SON, OUR LORD;

who was conceived by the Holy
   Ghost,
born of the Virgin Mary;
suffered under Pontius Pilate,
   was crucified, dead, and buried;
he descended into hell;
the third day he rose again from
   the dead;
he ascended into heaven,
and sitteth on the right hand of
   God the Father almighty;
from thence he shall come
   to judge the quick and the dead.

And in Jesus Christ,
his only Son,
our Lord . . .

1.

From Faith to Faith

This is a book about Jesus Christ.

It is rather presumptuous to write such a book. In the first place, suitable books are already available. The one by John in the New Testament, for example, is highly recommended. Indeed, no one would dare to add to or improve upon that book about the Christ— or could, even if he dared. And the other twenty-six in the New Testament must rank far above any other attempt. There is an authoritative and a qualitative gulf which cannot be bridged.

In the second place, as John himself says, no *book* can do the Christ justice. In fact, John doesn't think the world itself could hold the books necessary to describe our Lord completely (John 21:25). With this dash of poetry, John requires more than can ever be realized. And here the editor limits us to 115 pages!

There is even the chance that one more book will only add confusion.

The Risk

You, the reader, and I, the author, are embarked on an adventure that has a risk. Why do it?

There are at least two reasons.

1. Christians are compelled by the very nature of their relationship to the Christ to think, speak, write, and preach about him. Their response to him is such that they find it necessary to give expression to the meaning and significance that he has for them. They simply must live *for* him and talk *about* him. Silence is the symptom of an absence of faith. Indeed, it is only in this life of discipleship that one gets to know him at all. Books like this one are necessary even at the risk of being inadequate or troublesome.

The greater risk would be that men stop talking and listening—even stop arguing. For then faith would be dying on the earth

2. The Christ must always be talked about in language that is meaningful to the person talking. Even though John's Gospel is both unsurpassable and sufficient, it is *John's* Gospel. That is, it is the words of John, speaking out of John's experience, unique as it is, using the words of his day and time. Mark spoke as sufficiently, and so did Matthew and Luke. We are obligated to discover which words speak meaning-

fully and, of course, correctly of the same Christ for our time and place.

Just as a Christian community of long ago found the Apostles' Creed to be right for their confession, and another community several centuries later thought it necessary to use the words of the Nicene Creed, and as Luther, much later, expressed his faith in the Small Catechism, so we must discover the best way for speaking out of our concerns and with our presuppositions.

This in no way suggests that the Christ changes or that truth is relative but rather that language changes. Men's understanding of the world changes, and men themselves change in superficial but still important ways.

The news about the Christ must be kept clear, sharp, and meaningful, even if it takes many books—and some risk.

The marvelous thing is that we may find it possible to discover meaning in all of these other ways of speaking and yet speak powerfully ourselves in yet another way.

The purpose of this book is, therefore, not really to prove anything or even to provide solutions to knotty problems. Nor is there any claim that we can speak in a better way than those who have gone before us. We seek, rather, to witness to the Christ with a language that has been meaningful to many in this generation in order that a response may come from you, the reader.

There are several kinds of responses which we might provoke:

1. You may become angry.
2. You may be bored to tears (just an expression, you understand).
3. You may show mild interest and wonder why you bought the book.
4. You may become excited—in one of several degrees.

The best options are, of course, *1* and *4*. If you are miffed, it most likely is because (a) this book is wrong and you are right about something and your sense of justice is nettled, or (b) this book is right and you have been wrong and your conscience bothers you to the point that you have become defensive. In either case, you are likely to do something about it—such as doing some further investigating.

Which is good. Which is also why we have a short list of books in the back.

And if *4* should be your response, the same thing is likely to happen—you will do something, because nobody can be excited about Jesus Christ and remain silent. You may tell others about him—and excite them! It has happened before.

You need not make any promises or predictions at this point. When you finish, we will ask you to check your reaction. In fact, you can send it to us. Which may cause more, fewer, or different books to be written.

The risk belongs to both of us.

History and/or Faith

We said a moment ago that we speak in the language of faith. We could have approached our subject differently. It would have been possible to do a historical investigation attempting to determine the relationship between actual historical events and the New Testament writing about those events. There is merit in this if the purpose is to assemble historical facts about our Lord or to argue some point with a challenger. But it is not very helpful and can even be misleading if our purpose is to elicit or enlighten faith. The New Testament itself firmly resists this kind of investigation as a validation or proof of faith.

It is quite clear that the New Testament is a book written out of faith, too. Every author writes after his experience of faith. His purpose is to describe the faith. His hope is to engender faith in his reader.

In the process of proclaiming the Gospel, which is the same as proclaiming the Christ, the New Testament becomes deeply involved in history. This is because the Gospel is about something which happened in history and most specifically, of course, about the events in the life of a man, Jesus of Nazareth. But it is not the "bare" facts alone which constitute the Christian faith but those facts seen in a particular way. "Jesus is Lord" is an example of a statement which is significantly different from the historical fact "Jesus is a carpenter's son from Nazareth." The second phrase is the kind of fact which can be ascertained by a scientific investigation of the evidence. "Jesus is Lord" is a statement of faith which involves the acceptance of an interpretation of history not subject to the same kind of investigation. It is the interpretation which gives the final shape to faith.

Peter was quite aware that Jesus was a real historical figure. He was not concerned about historical criticism, nor did he have to think about establishing the historical facts about the Christ. He had been an eyewitness. But it was not until it dawned on Peter that these very events unfolding before his eyes pointed to Jesus as Messiah, an idea not necessarily evident to everyone seeing them, that anything like faith came to him. Only then did Jesus say "Blessed are you, Simon Bar-Jona! For flesh and blood has not revealed this to you, but my Father who is in heaven" (Matt. 16:17).

There is a rather strange wedding between history and faith in the New Testament. Although faith is rooted deep in real historical events, historical details and historical facts as we usually think of them with our scientific minds are not the chief concern of the New Testament writers.

Consider:

1. The date for the birth of Jesus is specific enough to be certain, but not specific enough to be datable on a calendar. Christmas, for example, is an arbitrarily chosen day. We are not even sure in which year A.D. we are living because we are not absolutely sure of the year of the star of Bethlehem.

2. The chronology of our Lord's life is rather vague

and a bit disoriented in the New Testament—we are not even certain of the length of his ministry or of his age at his death.

3. We do not have the slightest hint as to his physical features. Do not be confused by the portraits of him that you can buy almost anywhere. They are, whether good or bad art, solely the products of the imaginations of artists.

Sometimes the Gospel writers seem to make no effort at all to clarify historical details—and we are *so* curious. A good homework assignment to demonstrate this would be to compare the accountings of the resurrection.

1. Look up the four references: Matthew 27:55 to 28:20; Mark 15:40 to 16:20; Luke 23:49 to 24:53; and John 19:38 to 21:25.

2. Note especially the chronology, the places, and the persons involved.

3. List on a long sheet of paper the variances.

(There is more to this than a casual reading reveals—but wait until Chapter 5.)

Two dangers are apparent:

1. *That we confuse faith with acceptance of historical fact.* Theologians in the last century were tempted to do this. They tried to discover the facts "behind" the New Testament and in doing this, to recover the "historical" Jesus—which, they thought, would be the "real" Jesus. These scholars were excited about the

tools modern historical science had given them. This is understandable, for those methods were new and many unknown aspects of the Bible had been unearthed. Many scholars, however, did not reckon with the New Testament writers who knew a thing or two about the subject they were handling and the ways they chose to go about their business. Even today some well-meaning Christians are unduly occupied with proving the historical reliability of the New Testament. This is important of course, but the dangers must be recognized. Faith, in the New Testament sense, is trusting in a present living Lord and not simply accepting proven historical fact.

2. *That we confuse faith with ideas about God and reality without any foundation in history.* Faith would then become either a vague, mystical feeling or a philosophical system of a particular kind. As profound or as meaningful as this might seem to some, a faith without a historical base would not be the New Testament faith either. This happens, by the way, to be the most current danger in theology.

Have you ever wondered to which danger you are inclined?

The New Testament interprets history. We cannot always separate factual history from interpretation of history. Sometimes historical events themselves are used by the New Testament writers to interpret history. Mark is a classic case. Sometimes the New Testament uses speculative thought to describe Christ with history as a silent background and source. Paul is adept at this—consider Romans, for example.

Obviously both history and interpretation belong to the life of faith. To isolate one from the other is not only dangerous but impossible.

We actually have no real choice if we wish to be faithful to the New Testament. We have to speak from faith to faith.

Perspectives for Faith

But wait a minute! Let us not get too involved with the question of method, as important as it may be. It is also necessary to notice that the New Testament is very much aware of something we choose to call perspectives. That is, different writers of biblical books look at the Christ from different angles. They approach their subject in different ways, for different purposes, and with different styles and emphases.

The biblical writers share one basic perspective— they are all writing after the resurrection. They tell the story after knowing the plot—although before the last chapter. They are not second-guessing but speak out of experience. But while they have this same time perspective, they fasten their eyes on different aspects of the Christ, and use somewhat different vocabularies in their description, even to the point of using somewhat different names and titles for Christ.

It should become clear immediately that the resurrection will be very important for our study.

A chronological diagram of our thesis might look like this:

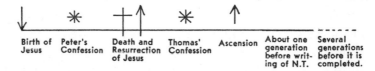

| Birth of Jesus | Peter's Confession | Death and Resurrection of Jesus | Thomas' Confession | Ascension | About one generation before writing of N.T. | Several generations before it is completed. |

The first three Gospels differ from each other in some respects, but they are alike in that they climax their presentation of the Christ by recording Peter's great confession which occurred before the crucifixion (Matt. 16:16, Mark 8:29, Luke 9:20). Their method is straight historical narrative through which they describe the Christ and his deeds, the nature of faith, the ways of God, the hope for the future, and many, many other events and ideas.

John, with a pronounced difference in style and vocabulary, climaxes his Gospel with the confession of Thomas in the risen Lord (John 20:24-29). Jesus says (and these words seem aimed right at us and *our* perspective), "Blessed are those who have not seen and yet believe" (John 20:29). John is interested more in relating a series of themes than in writing a biography of our Lord. He is really not too much interested in chronology except in a general way and moves from one area of discussion to another in essay style rather than through a strict recording of succeeding events.

Paul's style cannot be as neatly defined, but he seems little interested in historical facts except as anchors to hold down the faith — such as his great emphasis upon the cross and the resurrection in 1 Corinthians 15. For him the stress is upon the way of salvation—the action of the Holy Spirit in the present directing us back to what God has done in the past. Paul thus concentrates on great ideas almost altogether.

Now, these suggestions of differing approaches may seem to make the New Testament a diverse and disconnected book. Even faithful Christians who really begin to know this book for the first time and, therefore, to see these things, may be a bit bewildered. They had not realized before that the New Testament is a series of mountain peaks rather than a flat plain. Rising from the same base, each writer views the Christ from a different point on the horizon. We who view the Christ from a still different spot in time tend to see the peaks as different heights. John appears to be tall and stately, towering in literary style and theological depth. Mark is more blunt and rough with rugged strength. Matthew has more detail with long, sloping sides fading into the distance. Luke has a lovely peak, with many colored hues, graceful and softer. Paul is a series of peaks of varying shapes, sometimes angry and fuzzy, sometimes extending into the clouds above.

There is no doubt but that all the peaks have one converging point. Jesus Christ is the unity to which they witness. All kinds of things may vary, but the subject is the same. It is as though the writers are singing one melody but in various moods, at various tempos and even with quite different arrangements.

What is perhaps most significant of all is that, although the Christ is presented again and again with adequacy, that is, adequate for faith, no book, nor all of them together, "capture" the Christ fully. They rather "point" to him or "sing" about him, somewhat like this:

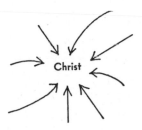

To all of this must be added *our* perspective of faith. The biblical writers wrote out of a common experience in a common time and out of rather common presuppositions. We can be sure that their testimony hits the mark. This is why they are the "apostolic" witness— the authoritative witness. Although each is unique, that is, his own, each is a true witness, and all other interpretations and perspectives must be modeled after them.

Our perspective is different. Consider these facts:

1. Most of us are not Jews and do not have the intimacy and feel of a long history.

2. We are not even from the Near East. Everybody knows, and Americans even are boastful of the fact, that Americans think in their own peculiar way. So did, and do, the peoples of that region of the world.

Their language has peculiar properties and their understanding of time, history, and person is unique.

3. We live in the twentieth century, not the first. In our day, even father and son have different thought patterns and frames of reference. What a gap there must be between the first and the twentieth centuries!

4. We are deeply influenced by a host of things. *(a)* The development of modern science and its understanding of the world makes us very literal and logical in our approach to truth. *(b)* By our knowledge, thanks to public school education, of many diverse philosophies and ideologies, our minds are cluttered, perhaps without our knowing it, by many concepts completely foreign to the biblical writers. We tend to read these ideas into the Bible or to judge the biblical witness by these extraneous standards. *(c)* We are accustomed to a way of life called democracy, which assumes certain ideas of justice, individual rights, economic theory, and ethical notions which could, and sometimes do, make it difficult for us to understand the precise point under discussion in the New Testament.

We have a problem! It is a miracle that we can be Christians at all—and that is as it should be. Remember the words of Jesus to Peter? Peter, too, had to be led into a wholly new way of thinking.

Patterns of Faith

The richness and variety, the diversity and unity, in the New Testament have been both a joy and a concern for Christians in the whole history of the Church. Who is this Christ? What figure of faith emerges out of this marvelous—and mysterious—book? Certain patterns of faith can be detected in Christian history.

The church in its first seven centuries or so was particularly concerned about understanding the human and the divine about Jesus. How shall we talk about Jesus in his relationship to God, they asked themselves. Three stages occurred in their discussion.

1. The Apostles' Creed, the earliest universally accepted and "complete" confession, seems determined to establish the humanity of Jesus. He was, it said:

conceived by the Holy Ghost
(by the Holy Ghost, yes, but really conceived, that is, with a biological history the same as everybody else after conception)

born of the Virgin Mary
(coming into the world through a woman as all men do)

suffered under Pontius Pilate
(with all the senses, even pain)

was crucified
(subject to the problems of government, justice, evil, as are all men)

died
(the mark of all men)

and was buried.
(dust to dust . . .)

Whatever else Jesus was, he was a man who shared the joys and the predicaments of men.

2. The Nicene Creed, in a second evolving pattern of faith, makes sure that the divinity is not neglected:

> God of God, Light of Light, very God of very God,
> begotten, not made,
> being of one substance with the Father . . .
> came down from heaven . . .

Has this language ever been surpassed?

3. Having established this as a way of speaking of our Lord, the church moved to define, at a meeting at Chalcedon in 451 (the church had many meetings then, too), how to speak of the relationship between the human and the divine in what was called the Chalcedonian Formula.

> We confess one and the same Son, our Lord Jesus Christ,
> perfect in Godhead, perfect in Manhood,
> truly God and truly man,
> of one substance with the Father . . .
> of one substance with us . . .
> one and the same Christ, Son, Lord, only-begotten,
> confessed in two natures, unconfusedly, inconvertibly,
> indivisibly, inseparably. . . .

In other words, the church was deeply involved in questions about the person of Christ. The question "Who was Christ?" was in the forefront. The doctrine dealing with Christ's nature or being is called the incarnation.

Another pattern of faith came into being in the Middle Ages and the Reformation—from about 1000 to 1700 A.D.—again about seven centuries. Here the question changed to "What did he do?" A scholar named Anselm in 1098 wrote his still famous little book on

Why did God become man? The Reformation, which influences us very much, as does Anselm, stressed the importance of the fact that "To know Christ is to know his benefits." The emphasis was upon the acts or works of Christ, and especially upon the cross.

Fortunately this discussion was not as complicated (perhaps the church is learning) and no creeds of the type originating in the early church were formulated —although we have various interpretations in the confessions of particular church bodies. But it was clear that a shift had occurred and the Christ was seen to a greater degree than before in terms of the salvation he offered. Certain stages in the thinking emerged here too—and this becomes the subject for Chapter 4 when we consider the doctrine about the atonement.

It is more difficult to describe briefly the content of the next great step, which is our modern era, because we are still in it. The question of history and faith which we touched on has been a very dominant theme—and still is—but I suspect that those who look back will see us as the "eschatological" age (what a word— maybe the church has not learned to be simple after all), that is, the age preoccupied with the question of the "goal" or "end" of God's work in Christ. It relates our Lord to the "wholeness" of things, and therefore involves such matters as nature, the judgment, the non-Christian world, the conclusion of history, etc. It sounds fascinating, and it is. We will talk about it in Chapter 6.

In some ways we have bitten off more than we can chew. We said, you remember, that we were being a bit presumptuous. We shall have to be very conscious of these patterns of faith if we are to be responsible. But anything interesting is worth some effort—and some risk.

So, let us launch out together.

Who was conceived by the Holy Ghost,
Born of the Virgin Mary . . .

2.

The Mystery of the Beginning

This is not a mystery story of the cloak and dagger variety. But it is a mystery nevertheless. There is no secret logical puzzle here that will be suddenly revealed on the last page, except perhaps at the end of history. Yet there is mystery in the sense that we are dealing with something too large for us. No matter how much we explain or define, there is always something left over or something which somehow does not seem to be just right. It is true, after all, that God does not fit into our ways of speaking or even understanding. We cannot capture him in a sentence or a concept. We *can* talk intelligently about the Christ, but we cannot *explain* him through the use of our intelligence.

The mystery is compounded because in Jesus we are dealing with God and man at one time. It is difficult enough to try to define man (what is the "I" for example?). And God, as Luther reminded us, is inexpressible. What, then, if we try to put the two together and with only one example to go by?

This is our task. The Christian faith declares that Christ is and was God and man. He is one who came from God and yet is one of us.

A Presupposition or Two

In order to get a toe hold on our task we need to take note of a presupposition. The Bible assumes that history is chronological. Of course, history is more than this, and we shall see later that the Bible has more than one understanding of time. But for now it is necessary to emphasize the reality of history. History is not an illusion. It is not cyclical or cynical. That is, it does not repeat itself endlessly without purpose. Time permits novelty. There can be something new under the sun. History can progress, have stages, and have a beginning and an end. It can also deteriorate and destroy its capacity for the purpose.

In trying to find ways to speak about the mystery of Christ, some Christians have analyzed the "stages" of Christ's person and work. They have said that the Christ is involved in three consecutive stages, and these are given the name "states." A diagram would look like this:

Pre-existence   Humiliation   Exaltation

Birth   Cross Resurrection

The state of pre-existence refers to that "time" before the incarnation, that is, the birth of our Lord. The state of humiliation is the name given to his life on earth. After the death and resurrection, Christ assumes the state of exaltation.

The idea of progression in this diagram is quite important. Christ does not, for example, return to God *after* the resurrection in such a way as to assume the same state that he had *before* the incarnation. He has a new state of being called exaltation. He is Lord, and this is not the same kind of existence as pre-existence. Furthermore, he is still the Incarnate One. That is, his birth into the world as a man is never erased and his humanity is never changed into some other kind of reality. Once it has happened, the incarnation cannot be undone or reversed.

Wow!

He is man forever!

That gives each aspect of the picture of the Christ greater importance. The incarnation and the cross as well are not just single events in a stream of other events, but are historical acts which change everything which happens in the succeeding chapters of history. This means that Christ can be something entirely new and unique—which would not be possible if history were always a repetition of something in the past.

In this chapter we want to concentrate on the beginning. We shall follow, logically, in the next chapters with a discussion of the humiliation, the cross or atonement, and the exaltation.

But first a brief word about pre-existence. Literally, of course, this means "before he exists." One could say "his existence before his existence," but this is rather confusing. The word existence, in current philosophical language, refers to life in the world of time and space, that is, creaturely existence. The Christian is one who believes that Jesus came from God and was with God before his birth into the world, by whatever name this ought to be called—and we really do not have a good word for it. This belief is terribly important because it is the foundation for the doctrine of the Trinity.

About this life we know nothing. John says: "In the beginning was the Word, and the Word was with God, and the Word was God. He was in the beginning with God . . . " (John 1:1, 2a). We cannot add to this, except perhaps to clarify that the word Word here refers to Christ. We know this from a verse further down in this same chapter (v. 14) which says simply (and profoundly), "The Word became flesh and dwelt among us."

A man named Arius in the third century thought he could expand a bit on this. He tried to interpret the biblical usage of the terms "Father" and "Son" very literally. He insisted that these words meant that God, the Father, spawned the Son before the creation of the world at a particular time. His theme was: "There was a time when he was not." But the church said no. This was an instance when a too literal interpretation of the Bible was considered heresy. Instead, the church said that the imagery of "Father and Son" was an idea taken from human life, and good as it was, could not be applied exactly to God. The Father and the Son have a continuous relationship of mutual love and dependence and there was no moment when the Son was created before the world was created. The Father "eternally generates" the Son. The idea of chronological time thus has limits. It is possible to speak of a time "before" history began. Already the suggestion is made that there may be another "kind" of time!

And so the Nicene Creed says:

> . . . begotten, *not* made.

But we are ahead of our story.

Humanity and Divinity

Jesus Christ is fully man and fully God. The word "fully" is a key word. He is not part man and part God, nor is he man some of the time and God some of the time, nor is he somewhere in between.

The great temptation is to overemphasize one idea or the other.

Jesus Christ is true man. As the Book of Hebrews bluntly reminds us (Heb. 2:17), he is like us in every respect, except that he did not sin. (Did I detect a raised eyebrow?) Perhaps we must say it again. He is like us in *every* respect—except that he did not sin. He shared in the wholeness of our life—its joys, its limitations, its pain, frustration and fright, its tiredness, its growing up, its desires and instincts, and its life with God.

He was born into this world as a baby, as any other baby is born. He grew up in a home with all the trials of any upbringing. He learned life through experience. He suffered and died, as really and truly as any of us will suffer and die.

This claim is stark and unmovable. To deny it is to blaspheme him, for it is to his glory that he is man. To detract in any way from the glory of his humiliation would be to destroy the Christian faith, because it would destroy the reality of the redemption. For if God did not become man, truly, there is no salvation. Indeed, it is through the acts of this man that salvation was accomplished.

He was so much man that, in a sense, he is the only true man that ever lived. The rest of us have fallen from humanity, but he exhibits the fullness of man in the midst of a fallen world.

It is almost impossible to stress his humanity too much. What becomes dangerous is to stress *only* his manhood. In the early church a community of believers called the Ebionites stressed his humanity very nearly to the exclusion of his divinity. You will occasionally see the term Ebionitic in theological writings even in our day. It refers to the tendency to be so interested—and this may be very pious—in the humanity of Jesus that the importance of his divinity is overshadowed and thus not properly understood.

Some Christians tried a sort of "half-way" approach. It was then, as it is now, very tempting to choose the middle of the road when facing difficult questions. They said that he was a true man and that God descended upon him at the time of his Baptism. The Holy Spirit

did descend upon him, as you will remember (Mark
1:9-11). And, they continue, he was the true man from
whom God retreated at the cross, which is indicated by
the words of Jesus himself in the cry "My God, my God,
why hast thou forsaken me?" (Mark 15:34). God
adopted this man Jesus for this critical period. Those
who think in this way are called adoptionists—which is
logical. But of course, what they are really doing is relating Jesus to God only part of the time and thus making his manhood his most important aspect.

Sometimes good and proper Christian talk uses language which sounds very much like an adoptionist
view. Take Luther's hymn "A Mighty Fortress" (a mighty
hymn, too). The second stanza of one translation goes
like this:

> Did we in our own strength confide
> Our striving would be losing;
> Were not the right Man on our side,
> The Man of God's own choosing.
> Dost ask who that may be?
> Christ Jesus, it is he;
> Lord Sabaoth his Name,
> From age to age the same,
> And he must win the battle.
>
> SBH 150:2

Note the emphasis upon "man" and "choosing."
Sounds rather like an adoptionist view, does it not?
But it is not. The difference between the correct and
the incorrect way of speaking is that the correct way
always associates God's choosing with the beginning
of the life of Jesus and always assumes the choice to
have permanent consequences.

Jesus Christ is also true God. He is "God with us." He is not just like God, or imbued with the spirit of God, or someone behaving as a God (how awful that would be). He *is* God. He shares in the very being and reality of God.

This is a frightening thing to say. If it were not true, the idea would be the work of the devil.

But if he is not God, then we have all been deceived and there is no salvation—the same consequences if he were not man.

It is quite possible to go astray on this one, too. And we have probably all done so in one way or another. The claim is the crux of the faith, and it is only in faith that it can be said at all. It is a confession and therefore not subject to final proof or disproof in this life. But it can be talked about and safeguarded—and even speculated about.

There are wrong ways to think about his divinity. One can stress his divinity to the exclusion of his humanity—which would be heresy. In fact, some early Christian communities thought of Jesus as a kind of ghost. He "seemed" like a man but he really was not, they said. They were, and are, called docetists—which comes from a Greek word which means "to seem." They were really quite pious—but piety does not necessarily produce truth. They thought Jesus was so wonderful that he could not possibly be a man. Evidently they did not think much of men.

And I suspect that this is our greatest temptation, too, surprisingly. We have talked so much about man and sin that we are a bit afraid to think of Jesus in the same breath with man. We tend to play it a little safe and tip the scales on the side of God, as it were

If we do, we blaspheme.

There are the half-way temptations here, too. What, said a man named Apollinaris, if we say that his soul and body were human but his spirit (perhaps we would say the "I") was divine? Sounds neat—as an eight-year-old would say—but in this scheme it is the "I" which is the real person, so Apollinaris was in the final analysis tempted to docetism.

The Nicene Creed nailed it down hard.

". . . being of one substance with the Father . . . and was made man . . . . "

The word substance, as it is used here, does not mean, as it usually does today, the "materialness" of something. It means rather "the power to continue to be." Whatever it is that makes something what it is was called the substance. Whatever God is, therefore, that Christ also was. Not similar substance, mind you, but the same substance. This is rather a good way to say it, because no precise understanding of God is necessary —indeed it is the other way around—we see God's substance in Christ.

One Undivided Life

Even if you and I should be able to maintain this double emphasis upon God and man, there remains still the most difficult part of all. How do we understand these two together?

One of the greatest temptations is to think of the Christ as being two entities—two things, as it were—put together. One great early Christian named Nestorius supposedly thought this way—and so there was born the heresy called Nestorianism. The solution is simple, he said (and right there you can get suspicious). Mary, the Mother of Jesus, being human, could not have been the Mother of God, he maintained—really a very sensible premise. This is especially so since the Word, John's name for the pre-existent Christ, you remember, "was" before Mary was even born. So, and the conclusion follows ever so logically, Mary must be the mother of only the "human side" of our Lord, and the "divine side" was joined to the human side at conception. The Christ, therefore, must be thought of as two separate natures joined together, like two boards glued together —with a good glue, of course.

But the church said no. The Council at Chalcedon in 451 A.D. formulated an answer that still stands as the classic definition of the incarnation. The Christ, said Chalcedon, and so do we, is one undivided life.

He is:

1. *One*. That is, we must not think of him as two "things" but as one person. More technically, he is one person with two natures. Using some of the language from John's Gospel, the church fathers conceived of it in this way.

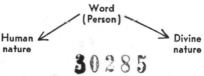

The Word was called a "person." Person is not a word in the Bible—the closest word is soul. But it does make some kind of sense to us, as it did to men in the fifth century, to think about the concept person as a usable one to communicate the essential meaning of Word. The Word, they were trying to say, the motivation, the moving force in God which wished to communicate itself to man, entered into an existence which we call human nature. In so doing, it did not discard or decrease or change its own divine nature, but at the same time it became human nature. The Word assumed human nature in such a way that a single person was related to two natures or substances—in the way we just defined substance.

2. *Undivided.* This "one person–two natures" being is so constituted that the two natures have a very special relationship. To describe this relationship, Chalcedon chose four adverbs—unconfusedly, inconvertibly, indivisibly, inseparably. These famous adverbs are really the heart of the matter (perhaps we should say substance). Christ is God and man in such a way—and Chalcedon made no claim to know "how"—that neither the godhood nor the manhood is diminished or changed by the presence of the other. Each is maintained separately, yet not in a way that one could presume to distinguish between them, and this is permanent—in fact forever, as we said.

3. *Life.* All these words are not meant to describe a chemical reaction, or a vague idea, but a living, dynam-

ic person. These are philosophical words attempting to communicate a life.

It is a big job. In fact, the Chalcedonian attempt does not quite manage it either, but none has done it better, so we have kept these words. They have blessed generations before us, so will bless us, too. Their chief purpose is not to explain but to protect the mystery by denying the wrong attempts to explain. They are not answers so much as safeguards of the faith and words of praise.

Other words are possible, however, because no life can be encompassed in one set of words, especially if words change their meaning. In our day it is popular to think about the incarnation as a paradox. A paradox is a truth that contains two contradictory or mutually exclusive ideas, both of which are necessary to communicate the truth and both of which are part of experience. To put it more bluntly, there are some things in life that do not seem to add up when viewed only from the perspective of common sense, but we sense that they are true nevertheless. Paradoxes are really quite common in life, especially in the inner or emotional life. It is possible to be both happy and sad at the same time, to hate and love the same person. In theology we call faith a paradox because we assert that God saves us and at the same time we know that it is necessary for man to believe. Faith is both a gift and a personal act. Perhaps, upon reflection, you will decide that most things in life that really count, that are ultimate, involve us in paradoxical thought—especially if we try to articulate their meaning in words.

The incarnation, some would say, is like that. The human and the divine exist together in this life, although it is logically impossible for them to do so. These scholars think that other words, such as nature and substance, do not help very much.

Some other current scholars dislike the terms substance, nature, and person altogether, saying that these words are outmoded and too philosophical and therefore, to them, too fuzzy for use. In fact, some people even consider them misleading. They prefer clear, sharp ideas such as the ones scientists supposedly use. These theologians want to emphasize the dynamic aspects of Christ more than the substantial aspects. "God is working through Christ" seems to them a more palatable way to relate God and man in Christ. Luther might even belong to this camp. There certainly is evidence that Paul sometimes preferred to think this way. It is rather difficult, however, to know whether the abandonment of such great words of long ago as substance and nature would help very much. Scientists do not always speak as clearly as they themselves think they do. In our day words like paradox, contradiction, mystery, and the like are creeping into their language too. It is really not necessary for us to make hard decisions about this in order to be faithful to the Bible. Indeed, flexibility and variety at this point are more in keeping with the diversity of the New Testament.

But back to our subject. The answer to Nestorius was

that Mary *is* the God-bearer. She did not create God (how foolish), but she bore the God-man. Therefore, rightly understood and without dispelling the mystery, she can indeed be called "Mother of God."

At this point we must put the virgin birth in its proper perspective. This aspect of the mystery of the incarnation has been badly handled and badly misunderstood in recent years.

Briefly the situation is this:

1. The traditional understanding is that a young woman became pregnant without having had intercourse with a man.

2. It is also our teaching (and here some disagree, such as Roman Catholics and some of our own church fathers) that the gestation period and the birth itself of Mary's child were normal and that she subsequently had other children by Joseph. Her virginity was limited to the conception of her firstborn child.

3. There are only two places in the New Testament which attest to these traditions—Matthew 1:18-25 and Luke 1:26-38. Although both John and Paul strongly affirm the mystery of the incarnation, they do not refer to the virgin birth.

4. Some biblical scholars challenge the authenticity of these two texts, claiming that they are not part of the original writings of the New Testament but were added as a part of the growing legend in the early Christian community in order to emphasize the uniqueness of

the Lord. These scholars are not attacking the divinity of our Lord, for they maintain that this has better witness in teachings other than the virgin birth, but they are making certain historical judgments regarding the biblical text as they honestly see the evidence.

5. Some theologians have insisted that the virgin birth must be true for theological reasons—that is, Jesus could not have been God and man if he had been conceived in the usual way. The Word, they say, could have assumed human nature only in a way that was different from the ordinary origins of life.

And briefly, too, our view is:

1. The authenticity of the biblical texts has not been challenged to the degree that requires us to abandon the universal Christian tradition at this point. Of course, we must all realize that the nature of the subject is such that it is really beyond historical verification or even investigation. The view concerning the nature of the authority of Scripture also enters in. Our discussion about history and faith in the first chapter gives us the consistent right to say that the text *as given* is our authority whether or not the historical origins can be ascertained and whether or not the documents as we have them originated with one writer or developed to the present stage through a series of editings.

2. Some of our venerable church fathers exceeded *their* authority in virtually demanding that God had to

become man in a certain way. In their zeal to be faithful, they became enamored with the idea that they had grasped the necessary way for God to act in order to become incarnate. Nonsense! If we have, as men, somehow misinterpreted the conception of Jesus, this does not mean that the incarnation did not happen. The way Jesus was conceived neither proves nor disproves, neither explains nor makes more intelligible, the incarnation.

3. The point of the Christian tradition is that Jesus Christ is a unique event in history. He is not the product of purely natural forces, as we all are. He did not arise out of an orderly process as a sort of climactic gift of nature. He is the intervention of God in history. Jesus was generated by God's Spirit. How, exactly, God arranged this we may not fully understand, but it is our faith that he did so. The tradition of "conceived by the Holy Ghost, born of the Virgin Mary" says that very well and preserves that faith. The mystery is not solved by biology either.

One Undivided Life forever!

What Does This Mean?

That is a good question. And a necessary one. We suggested at the beginning of this book that Christians must talk in their own language—while, perhaps, at the same time understanding and using other language. Well, we have been analyzing, pretty much, other lan-

guage—the language of the 3rd, 4th, and 5th centuries
—with a touch of the 16th.

But what is the significance of this to a man in the
20th century? Can we talk about the meaning of Christ
for us? I think we can.

For example—and we shall not exhaust the subject:

1. God is in the realm of human experience. God is
not far away in some spiritual or supernatural world,
far from our life—if that is what supernatural means to
you. God is in the midst of life. He dwells with us. He
can be experienced.

Now, this is an important thing to say and know.
When Christians talk about their God they are not talking about the Wizard of Oz, even though sometimes it
may sound that way. Christians are confused sometimes, like everybody else. In fact, the only God Christians, or anybody else, have ever "seen" is the one
they see in Jesus Christ—and he is a man!

God is not just an idea, a hair-brained creation of
some "egghead"—he is presented as one who speaks
through someone like me. He is part of the very stuff
of life—of love and hate, of fear and hope, of blood
and sweat and tears, of birth and death.

To put it differently, God is terribly relevant to our
life in this present historical moment.

Indeed, God is so close and so available that it is
terrifying. How can you escape such a God?

2. God comes to us. The assumption is generally
made in popular religion that man finds God by search-

ing for him. No, says the traditional Christian. Man may yearn for God, but it is God who finds man. I did not discover God. He found me. The direction is from God to man.

And further he comes to me where I am. I do not have to leave this world, practice yogi, take leave of my senses, or desert my mind—or my wife. God comes to me in *my* humanity and in *my* history.

How can I escape him?

3. God comes to stay. He does not dip in and out of the human view like a flitting firefly. He is not coy or vague or playing a game. His stay is not temporary. He pledges himself to us forever. He has tied himself to us for all time.

How can I refuse to love him?

4. God reaffirms my humanity. There have been all kinds of views of man—some overoptimistic and therefore unrealistic and harmful—and some overpessimistic and therefore unrealistic and harmful.

The incarnation tells me two things about myself. *(a)* God values man as man and therefore me as me. What a tremendous compliment to man that God became one! How could he better demonstrate his concern for us? And how do I dare not to love all men? Indeed, how do I dare not to care for myself! Man becomes what God intended him to be by virtue of the incarnation. Suddenly my view of myself, other men, and indeed the world itself changes. This world has meaning. I am not a stranger here. This is my home until God arranges another. My life is something to cherish, to develop, to share, to honor. *(b)* God found it necessary to become man because men have lost their manhood. Why did God become man? Because men needed him. And in that there is a great indictment. Something radical had to be done. Something dreadful must be wrong. My life cannot be treated casually or indifferently. I must examine it and heal it. I am a man but only a man.

5. God knows me. He knows me well. He knows me inside out. He knows how I feel, how I fear, how I postpone, how deeply I love, how it hurts, and he knows even abandonment and accusation. I can trust him to help because he came to be like me.

Like me? How like me? And thereby hangs the tale of the next chapters.

3.
The Man for Others

The title of this chapter is the same as that of a book by Erik Routley.[1] Routley, as he explains, borrowed it from the title of the fourth chapter of a celebrated and controversial book *Honest to God* by J. A. T. Robinson, bishop of Woolwich.[2] The bishop, in turn, got the idea from the martyred German theologian, Dietrich Bonhoeffer, who in his *Letters and Papers from Prison* called the Christ a "man existing for others, and hence the crucified. A life based on the transcendent."[3]

This phrase has haunted me since I first read it in Bonhoeffer long ago. It struck me, as it must also have Routley and Robinson, as a most apt way to speak of the earthly life of our Lord. His was a life completely dependent upon God, completely given to others, a life joyful and triumphant but also sad and sorrowing, a life "obedient unto death" (Phil. 2:8).

We do not know as much about him as we would like. The New Testament gives us only glimpses into those few short years—some lovely stories about his birth, a fleeting glance into his very young manhood, and then a series of incidents taken from his public ministry, culminating in the great detail of his suffering and death.

We know so much and yet so little. It is not possible to reconstruct his life with any real adequacy. The New Testament forces us rather to see him as the object of faith. Its purpose is not to give us a newspaper account that would tempt us to live back in the first century in Galilee. Many have attempted to write the story of his life, and some of these have been useful and helpful, but all, in my opinion, have fallen short of their goal. And in a sense, the purpose has been wrong. The New Testament directs us to the resurrected Lord, not to the Nazarene. This does not mean that his life is not immensely instructive and magnificent in its force and example. It means only that we can do no more than what the New Testament itself does.

And it is clear that the New Testament hides some things from us. We cannot dissect Jesus' mind, for example. There are secrets there forever concealed from public view. When, in some critical moments, such as Gethsemane, his innermost heart is laid bare, it is almost too much for us and we could almost have hoped that those thoughts too could have remained hidden. His words from the cross are both terrifying and precious. In the Gospel of Mark there is the celebrated secret of his Messiahship. Without explaining his reasons, Jesus restrains his followers from making public their thoughts about his mission and is strangely reticent about accepting the title of Messiah.

But it is devastatingly clear that his life was dominated by the terror of love. Driven by a consuming passion to be obedient, he gave himself so utterly that they killed him. A man cannot give more than his life.

The Emptying

And here a question arises. Believing as we do in both his humanity and his divinity, how are we to assess the relationship between these two natures in his day-to-day life? From our perspective in the post-resurrection era, we already know the last act of the play and cannot "discover" his significance by living with him from the beginning as his disciples did.

A great deal of attention has been given to this question in the last century or so. The nature of the incarnation, as we have discovered, was dealt with extensively in the early church. In our modern era we have asked questions which arise within the basic commitment to the ecumenical creeds but go beyond them to new areas of concern.

Much attention has been centered on a verse in Philippians 2. There Paul says, "Have this mind among yourselves, which you have in Christ Jesus, who, though he was in the form of God, did not count equality with God a thing to be grasped, but emptied himself,

taking the form of a servant, being born in the like-
ness of men" (vv. 5-7). The question is, What does
"emptying" mean? Three main schools of thought
have come into being in answer to this troublesome
but fascinating question.

1. The first point of view is that emptying refers to
the incarnation itself. God, in deciding to come into
the life of men to redeem them, put aside the glories
of heaven. He did not, however, put aside either his
nature (and this is universally accepted) or the *powers
of that nature*. The emptying is a change of status but
not a change in essential character. That even God
cannot do, according to this approach.

This means, of course, that Jesus of Nazareth was
fully aware of who he was from the very beginning
and had within his grasp the full capacities of God the
Father. He knew all things, was all-powerful, and was
indeed not really subject to weakness or danger. Evidence for this view is found in the miracles, the seeming ability of Jesus to know the future, and generally
in the judgment that he controlled all things about
him. More basically, however, I think that this view
rests upon the assumption that God is unchangeable,
and that given the Chalcedonian understanding of the
incarnation, it would follow logically that Jesus was as
fully cognizant and able in his divine nature as he was
in his human nature.

Some who hold this view would say that there were
times when Jesus deliberately concealed his wisdom

and his power. At certain moments he voluntarily chose not to reveal or to use his divine abilities. He could not give them up, but he could refuse to use them. Still others suggest that he had these powers "potentially," that is, latent and within beck and call, but that he, except in extraordinary circumstances, did not use them and perhaps, indeed, was not constantly conscious of them.

This is a traditional view held by many Christians, and we must treat it with respect and care. But I find it difficult to find sufficient supporting evidence in the New Testament for it. Indeed, to me it suffers from too many docetic temptations.

2. A second opinion swings the pendulum to the other extreme. Those favoring this suggest that the emptying is a voluntary act of the second person of the Godhead *before the incarnation* and that consequently Jesus of Nazareth had no innate knowledge of his origin or even of his mission. He had the same powers that all men have (and no more). The wondrous things which he did grew out of the power which his dependency upon God gave him and which is available to every man. This does not deny his divinity. The classic understanding of the incarnation may still be held, but this view makes a sharp distinction between nature and the powers or attributes of nature. It is possible, say the proponents of this idea, to share in the nature of something (or someone) without also sharing in the capacities of that nature.

This was the case with Jesus. He was of the nature of God but, before his birth, had given up, emptied himself, of the powers of God. He deliberately made himself weak in order that he might redeem.

Those who believe this are well aware of the risks that God took by operating in this way. The temptations of the man Jesus were terrifyingly real. The Garden of Gethsemane was no sham. He conquered in his weakness, and this is his glory

Some within this pattern of thinking make a great deal of the secret of his Messiahship in Mark and maintain that Jesus never did accept the fact of his Messiahship. The title of Messiah was attributed to him by his disciples, but he went to his death in obedience, unaware of the real import of what was happening. We must realize that this is theoretically possible. It is not necessary for the efficacy of God's act of redemption that Jesus knew everything about what God was doing. The real question is not what kind of logic seems most helpful, but what does the New Testament really say?

My own judgment is that this view, too, leaves too many questions unanswered and too much evidence in the New Testament outside of serious consideration. We must go farther.

3. A third opinion states a bit more simply that we cannot answer the question of the emptying with complete clarity. There is sufficient mystery here to cause us to pause before making a final plunge into dogmatic

assertions. Certain aspects of the life of Christ seem to be somewhat clear and worthy of retention, however. The first is that Jesus grew and developed as a normal human being. He was not a ghost. His appearance among his fellows was not startlingly different from that of other men. He exhibited all the emotional, intellectual, and physical attributes of a man. He became angry, wept, was joyful, expressed puzzlement, was sorrowful, needed consolation, seemed to go from stage to stage in his thinking, parried questions, was disappointed, etc., etc.

Second, the understanding of his mission seemed to begin at a certain point in his life and steadily become more meaningful to him. Perhaps there is an embryonic beginning in the famous story of his trip to Jerusalem at the age of 12. It is difficult to be certain. But his Baptism was certainly a tremendous step in commitment to his mission. By the time of the decision to go to Jerusalem for that last fateful week, his mind appeared resolute, certain, aware. The struggle was not over, as evidenced by Gethsemane, but the goal was clear.

Third, there was no point at which he did not evidence a complete dependence on God the Father. He did not gather to himself his own power, even of decision. He relied upon his Father. He considered himself sent of God and in this way subordinate to him. "I do nothing on my own authority but speak thus as the Father taught me" (John 8:28).

And fourth, he evidenced on several occasions his

lack of full knowledge. The most famous example is his denial that he knew the time of the coming of the Son of Man (Matt. 24:36).

Without being willing to make precise philosophical distinctions, those who follow this interpretation, which relies heavily on the idea of progression and development in Jesus, would maintain only that New Testament evidence appears to substantiate the notion that the emptying of which Paul speaks does involve the giving up of the full powers of the Godhead without changing the essential nature of godhood. To what extent this happens and whether or not it is wise to be too precise remains questionable. It is clear only that the humanity of our Lord must not be endangered by pious demands on our part that he be "more" than human, nor must the divine nature be compromised to satisfy demands for clarity by curious minds.

The secret of Jesus' self-understanding remains his secret.

Signs of the Hidden

Even though we might have to hold the final question about the exact nature of the relationship between the human and the divine in abeyance, it is clear that there were many signs of the power which this man manifested.

For example, his authority was tremendous. He spoke as no man ever had among the Jews. What man before had driven money-changers out of the temple with a whip, made caustic criticisms of the powerful religious party of the Pharisees, cast out demons, defied Rome, overthrown the rules of the Sabbath, re-interpreted the whole law and the prophets, attributed prophecies to himself, sent out disciples with orders to judge the people, separated himself from his family with a rebuke to his mother, and spoken with such assurance that crowds followed him into the wilderness, tax collectors left their posts, prostitutes repented, fishermen left their nets, persecutors turned into preachers, and the representatives of Rome became troubled and even frightened?

But even more than this, he forgave sins. This was the most authoritative act of all in the eyes of the Jews. Only God could do this, and this Jesus of Nazareth did. Surely, no one can read more than a few pages of any of the Gospels before being struck by the extraordinariness of this prophet.

And, of course, there are the miracles. These acts of the Christ have been much discussed in our century. With a rather new view of nature given us by the scientific era, we have had to think again about how we should understand them. Some people have thought they could explain the miracles by applying their knowledge of how nature works, and thus they may have seemed to degrade the significance of the miracles. Others have insisted that the miracles are contrary to the workings of the laws of nature, but this view, too, has assumed a particular understanding of nature which may have more to do with twentieth-century thought than biblical thought. Still others have been chiefly concerned with some technical textual problems and have been led to judgments that seem to upset some traditional ideas.

One school of thought has insisted that the miracles are above criticism and that any attempt to analyze them too closely will endanger our faith in the god-hood of Jesus. They see the miracles as final proofs of his divinity and find comfort in the sureness with which the New Testament relates them.

The situation may not be as difficult as these various ideas suggest. Miracle is our word for those actions which the New Testament calls signs. Their relation to nature is a question which we have raised out of our environment and is not the New Testament's concern. Without understanding nature too well—and we are learning more and more about how little we know—and without having enough historical information to make final decisions in every case, we must rely upon the simple New Testament account and the *purpose* of the miracles in Jesus' ministry.

The first sign at the wedding at Cana gives us a clue. Here, John relates, Jesus did the first of his signs "and manifested his glory; and his disciples believed in him" (John 2:11). It is clear that John understood miracles to belong to the life of faith and that they were testimonies to the lordship of Christ. They do not present evidence which constitutes proof of this lordship and which can be finally ascertained and analyzed. They are signs which point away from themselves to the person who used them to teach of himself. Whatever the natural or historical details of a particular incident which we can call a miracle, there can be no doubt as to their point and goal. They reveal the hidden claim to his lordship and they call for the response of faith.

Other accounts of miracles in the New Testament are not all as clear as John's account about the miracle in Cana. We shall have to continue to learn from the Gospels as to what the full and true significance of miracle is. We know that the New Testament era was full of miracle men and magicians who fascinated their audiences with strange antics. Jesus was not one of these. Something deeper was called for than curiosity concerning the how.

Perhaps the most important thing of all was the content of his teaching. What he said and who he was are inseparable. His words to us in sermon and prayer and intimate talk with his disciples are not to be judged solely for their intrinsic wisdom and beauty. He did not come to give us a new philosophy and then leave us to live by this code of life. But his words pointed to God; they were signs in themselves of the hiddenness of his origin and power. They are part of the emerging pattern that we are examining that leads to the supreme confession of faith: He is Lord. The Sermon on the Mount is not the center of the New Testament, as some Christians seem to say, but they are words given to us as an authoritative witness of Jesus' being sent from God.

Learned Obedience

If there were signs of hidden power, there were also signs of weakness. "He can deal gently with the ignorant and wayward, since he himself is beset with weakness," Hebrews 5:2 reminds us in describing the qualifications of a high priest. Jesus was just such a priest. His glory is not revealed only in power but also in his willingness to subject himself to the predicaments which all men must endure. "Since therefore the children share in flesh and blood, he himself likewise partook of the same nature, that through death he might destroy him who has the power of death, that is, the devil, and deliver all those who through fear of death were subject to lifelong bondage" (Heb. 2:14, 15).

There is a helpful phrase in Hebrews 5:8, "Although he was a Son, he learned obedience through what he suffered . . . . " The clear biblical idea which we must vigorously maintain is that he shared so fully in our world that he shared our ignorance, our confusion, our temptations, our loneliness—indeed he even took our sin upon himself. His temptations, his sufferings, and his death were real—so real as to cause us to bow in shame and perhaps even to believe.

It is only when we have come to the point where this is a critical problem, where the contradiction between his hidden powers and his revealed weakness is resolutely unsolvable, that we see the significance of the mystery of the doctrine of the incarnation. The rather theoretical concerns of the relation between human and divine suddenly become starkly meaningful in the daily life of a single man from Palestine. He suffered in the world and time of Pontius Pilate.

He learned through this suffering. Through these experiences he grew to full stature. His claim to be our Savior was earned. There was nothing about his life that was a sham, pretense, play acting, or lacking in meaning. His life was not a series of motions which would be later revealed as only empty signs. His weakness was an aspect of his work of redemption.

The difference between him and us is that, although he suffered all things and indeed was tempted in all things, he endured. He conquered. He did not fall. He did not sin. His human nature in the final analysis was not precisely as ours, for we are sinners. He was unique. There is no other like him. But his claim to uniqueness was not given him from above as an unearned gift, but was a witness of his life itself.

And this is the greatest miracle of all. He was one of us but he knew no sin.

The famous verse in Philippians 2 is followed by these important words, "Therefore God has highly exalted him and bestowed on him the name which is above every name . . . and every tongue confess that Jesus Christ is Lord" (2:9-11). His weakness is also a testimony to his lordship, and his glory is also the glory of his humanity.

What Does This Mean?

There are more meanings than these two pages can encompass. But perhaps to step back and look at the larger aspects of the life of our Lord would be helpful. I suspect that the greatest danger here would be to concentrate on the trees rather than the forest. We shall look to the forest.

1. First, an important theological idea: God speaks to us *through* a man. The nature of God is not revealed through explicit concepts. God does not stand before us in his naked power and shining glory. No one has ever seen God. But we behold his glory in his Son, the Word made flesh, the man of Galilee. We see his glory through humanity. Having grasped this, we are able to understand many other aspects of the faith. The Bible, for example, is that human and weak instrument through which the witness of God comes to us. The Bible is not perfect and glorious in the way God is, but is a human witness by which he speaks to us. The church is a weak means by which he comes to us and dwells with us. God has chosen to work with us through the human. His power is made perfect through weakness. When we understand this, we can see the significance of the long and tortuous history of Israel, reconcile ourselves to the process by which the New Testament came into being, live in the sinful community called the church, and begin to worship our Lord.

And perhaps we shall even learn how to love our brothers in the human race. And this is our task.

2. We learn from the life of our Lord that to be a Christian is to be a man. This is another emphasis from Bonhoeffer but it ought to be everyone's interpretation of the New Testament. To be a Christian does not imply leaving aside some aspect of humanness. Christianity does not abandon the body and fly to a spiritual realm. A Christian grasps the fullness of life, faces the problems of his predicament, and abandons himself to the tasks of his time and place. Our Lord was a Jew with particular parentage, living in a particular town, with a given environment and an assigned task.

3. To be fully a man means to be fully dependent on God. To acknowledge the source of our being, to bow in humility before his judgment, to rally to his call for arduous tasks, to trust in his salvation—this is what it means to be a man. This is how we learn to be men—by obeying. This involves discipline, patience, and perhaps even suffering. This does not mean that God keeps us in tight reins, that life becomes burdened with rules, restrictions, and petty detail. God gives us freedom to make many decisions, he *trusts* us to live each moment with the power he gives us. He will not disparage us for our weakness but will use it to guide us. But if we depend solely on ourselves and relegate to ourselves the role of God, we lose our manhood.

This calling, of course, is too high for us. We shall

not be like him in this life. If we were able to be as fully dependent on God as Jesus was, we would need no Savior. But we sin and need forgiveness.

4. The life to be lived is one which is in the world and for others. The soul is the person and the person is part of a mankind with all its sociological, political, ethical, and intellectual implications. We cannot be other than men living in this year, in this nation, with this heritage, with these problems, and with these gifts. We cannot escape the world. We ought not to be identified with the world in the sense that we find our destiny and comfort in it, but we must be identified with the world in the sense that we are called to work in it, work for it, and suffer with it. Christ came into the world because he loved it, and he gave himself for it. This is our calling, too. We must learn, as he did, to be obedient through suffering.

Footnotes

[1]Erik Routley, *The Man for Others* (New York: Oxford University Press, 1964), p. xi

[2]J. A. T. Robinson, *Honest to God* (London: SCM Press, 1963), p. 64.

[3]Dietrich Bonhoeffer, *Letters and Papers from Prison* (London: SCM Press, 1953), p. 179.

4.
Pictures of a Death

This is the most important chapter in this book. Nothing else matters as much. The incarnation would not have fulfilled its purpose without Christ's death, and the resurrection and consequent exaltation would not have been possible. It is idle speculation to consider what would have happened if . . . . President Franklin Roosevelt used to refuse to answer "iffy" questions. In our situation here, it is impossible.

Jesus died for me.

This is the faith.

And this we must carefully examine.

In doing so, we expose the whole faith. God became man in order that . . . . He learned obedience in order that . . . . Everything begins and ends here. This is why Paul could say that he knew nothing except Christ crucified. What he meant, of course, was that he knew everything when he knew the meaning of Christ's death. Luther wanted his theology to be a theology of the cross, centered in the brokenness and victory of the cross, rather than a theology of glory, centered in heaven and claiming perfection and finality.

A Point of Departure

There are three elements involved in our discussion: (1) Because Christ is who he is, God is involved; (2) because Christ is who he is, man is involved; (3) because the world is what it is and Christ came into the world, sin and evil are involved. These basic elements must be arranged and related if we are to understand the significance of the atonement. And as we shall see, they can be interrelated in several different ways.

What the death of Christ accomplished must also be examined. The purpose, and the result, of his death is the atonement, that is, the salvation of men. God created men to be in fellowship with him, but that relationship has been obscured and perhaps even obliterated by sin and evil. The story of the Fall in Genesis 3 describes the origin and character of this broken relationship which envelops the whole human race. Man needs to be rescued or redeemed from his predicament. The death of Christ is the action which accomplishes this. Man is brought back to his original place as a creature trusting and depending upon his Creator.

How this is brought about is also an inevitable aspect of our study. Although, as we have already indicated, we are a bit skittish about claiming a full knowledge about God's ways with us, nevertheless we are able to examine the possibilities the New Testament offers us. Even if we do not achieve absolute clarity, we can discover the shape and character of God's greatest act. There is ample revelation for the assurance of faith.

We cannot take refuge in some easy formulations which the church has universally endorsed. The atonement is an aspect of the faith which has not been congealed into an authoritative dogma. The situation is quite different from that of the doctrine of the incarnation. There we had an accepted vocabulary to analyze and a long tradition to translate into our own language. The atonement, more meaningful to most Christians than the incarnation, has no carefully worked-out creed or confession. Strange, yet hauntingly right, this fact displays the church's recognition that here the mind must flutter in anxiety and the heart take over in the abandonment of faith.

There are several reasons for this lack of formal definition:

1. The New Testament offers several approaches to the interpretation of the atonement. Here the diversity in the New Testament that we discussed in the first chapter becomes significant. Several motifs run through both the Gospels and the Epistles. No one

has yet devised a single intelligible structure for these several interpretations that has become a universal creed. The atonement is like a jewel with many reflective facets, each shedding light on the whole, no one surface complete in itself and yet all necessary for the full brilliance of the gem.

2. The church has not yet had a crisis of such dimension that a final apologetic definition seemed necessary. In a sense, the atonement has needed no defense, at least not in the same way as the incarnation.

3. The church has managed in its long and tumultuous history to preach the message of the atonement in a way that was both true and relevant to each age. In the patristic period, the first five centuries or so, a particular aspect of the atonement was especially meaningful. The Middle Ages, 1000 to 1500 or so, chose a different but enormously fruitful approach. The modern era, 1800 to the present, has had its own favorite way of speaking, although since each succeeding age is the inheritor of the preceding times, the modern age has had a richness not altogether realized in any other era since the Apostolic Age. This is to say that although all motifs have always been present, they have not all been as influential as they are in our time.

Our duty, in light of this, is to analyze several interpretations—sometimes they are called theories or types—all of them rooted in the Bible and meaningful, current, and necessary. It would be possible to speak of as many as seven or eight approaches or theories, depending upon how carefully and closely distinctions are drawn. We shall stick to traditional procedure, however, and limit our discussion to three. This will bring into our study all of the essential elements and at the same time, we hope, reduce confusion. We shall speak of pictures of the atonement.

The Victor

The first picture we consider was dominant in the patristic period and was revived to become an influential theme in Luther, especially in his Small Catechism. It did not remain the most important interpretation in the centuries following Luther but has been emphasized again in our century as a result of new biblical research and new interest in the Reformation. There are a number of names attached to it—the classic picture (because it is old), the dramatic type (it certainly is that, as you will see), and the objective theory. We choose to refer to it as the Victory Picture (V.P. for short) because Christ is pictured as the Victor, the Conqueror for God.

Let us begin with a diagram. Diagrams can be misleading, and are never wholly convincing, but they provide an image to talk about and help us understand interrelationships. They also assist us in remembering differences.

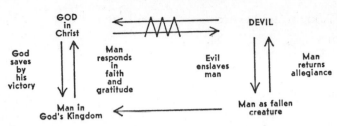

The world is the scene of conflict between God and evil, which is represented by the devil. In Christ God enters into the battle to defeat evil. He chooses to fight on the devil's own ground, the world of men. Men are enslaved by evil; their minds and hearts are darkened and their wills overcome; and they are helpless to rescue themselves from this prison. Through the life and death of Christ, God defeats evil, frees man, and puts man into the kingdom of God under his own kingly rule. Man is transferred from the slavery of evil to the freedom of the rule of God. Christ thus is pictured as the Victor over man's enemies, such as death, evil powers, and even man himself.

In every large city, on some small back street, you can find a little shop with three balls hanging from a side-arm outside. Everybody there knows that this is a pawnshop. Money can be borrowed by "hocking" some article of value. The shopkeeper holds the article until the loan is repaid (with high interest, we might add). During this time he has possession of the article, although he is not its rightful owner. He must give it back when it is redeemed, that is, when the price is paid for its freedom.

Some familiar sentences come to mind:

> . . . and to give his life as a ransom for many (Matt. 20:28).

> . . . you were bought with a price (1 Cor. 6:20).

> . . . God was in Christ reconciling the world to himself (2 Cor. 5:19).

> . . . bought and freed me . . . not with silver and gold . . . in order that I might be his and live under him in his kingdom . . . (Luther's explanation of the Second Article of the Apostles' Creed—an older translation).

> . . . From age to age the same,
> And he must win the battle.
>
> (Luther's Hymn "A Mighty Fortress")

This is colorful language, full of imagery and sometimes quite strange or even disturbing to a modern man. A student of language might call it "mythical" language. What does it convey? Note the following:

1. God is the total actor. Acting through Christ, he brings about his desired end by himself without depending upon anyone else. God and Christ are identical in the work. God has two problems. (It may be highly questionable to speak of God's problems, but remember that we are using human images to speak about an inexpressible God.) First, the presence of evil is a challenge to God. This evil has an existence of its own. It is not equal to God and its source is not in God. But seen from man's perspective within history, evil is in conflict with God. Second, man is enslaved by this power and needs to be rescued. God loves man and desires fellowship with him and acts to nullify the power of evil over man. Notice that it is not

suggested that God fights evil primarily to establish justice, important as that may be.

Hidden behind this dramatic picture of conflict and victory is the tension between holiness and love. God is both just and loving, and this might seem to be a problem too, as every parent knows. But the Victory Picture does not try to solve this tension—if it really is God's problem. The atonement, says this approach, does not probe into the unseen life of God. When God appears to us, he is either a God of wrath or a God of love. In the act of the atonement, God is solely love. He is pure grace. This is another way of saying that the atonement is the Gospel in its highest form.

2. Man is in the hands of powers greater than himself. He is caught in a whole host of things he cannot control—death, his own selfishness, ignorance, fleshly desires, hate, a cruel world, disease, etc., etc. Man here is really mankind, because man can only be understood in terms of his organic relationships to the whole human race. God deals with all of mankind in this act.

Man is that *for* which God acts, therefore, but he is not that *upon* which God acts. Man's role is that of a beneficiary of what God does in Christ and not a partner or even a participant in what is happening. Man is, as it were, "outside" of the atonement. The atonement is purely objective, that is, an event complete in itself and separate from man's personal involvement. Man watches with wonder from afar. Golgotha is too high for him.

3. Evil in the V.P. has cosmic, that is, universal con-
notations. Evil is not just a name for the sins which I
commit, such as lying, adultery, and selfishness, but it
denotes a power which grasps me. I am surrounded by
a world which has realities in it called evil. Evil is not
only "in" me but I am "in" a world of evil. In the
early church this idea was often expressed by the use
of very lurid imagery which spoke of demons, spirits,
and what not. To ancient people the world was haunted, and consequently most people were very super-
stitious. Christ, in a sense, saved them from their demonic superstitions. It is not necessary for us to think
in this way. In fact, it would be harmful to invent demons in order to be saved from them. We live in a
world which has its own powers of evil. Our world is
haunted by mushroom clouds, genocide, dope addic-
tion, racism, brainwashing, jealousy, etc., etc. Whole
societies are grasped by demonic-like ideas which in-
flict misery and death upon millions of people who
do not believe in devils. The devil is as real as sin. Redemption has to do, not just with me, says the V.P.,
but with my existence, which means my whole environment, the world in which I live.

4. Salvation is something which God does. Having
already happened at the cross, salvation is locked in
the past. Words like finished, accomplished, and unchangeable can be used of it. Salvation is atonement.
Atonement is salvation. Seen from man's perspective,
salvation is freedom. Man is transferred from one

world into another world—from slavery to freedom, from death to life, from hopelessness to great possibilities. A new orientation to everything results, a new humanity is born.

5. How can this happen through the death of a man, even through the God-man? The V.P. does not say. Its purpose is not explanation but description. According to this approach, the atonement can only be asserted, not argued. In a sense, then, this is an irrational interpretation of the atonement—there is no attempt to engage one's interest by a logical argument, by touching upon one's sympathies or psychological experience or even by appealing to the character of the world. Of course, one has hints—the temptation by the devil was overcome, the miracles demonstrated victories over man's enemies, and the resurrection is a necessary corollary of the death to demonstrate the character of the victory, but the how is really never very satisfactorily explained. It can be readily seen that the effort cost God a great deal. He sacrificed his Son. Sometimes there is discussion as to who received the ransom, and much needless argument has adorned the pages of noted books by learned theologians. The ransom, of course, was paid to no one. Just as an American soldier at Iwo Jima sacrificed his life for his country and thus paid a ransom, so Christ gave his life. The Japanese did not receive the G.I.'s life, nor did his country. The words sacrifice and ransom in this context are ways of speaking of cost and are not meant to convey the meaning of transaction or exchange of value.

. . . not with silver or gold, but with his holy and precious blood . . . (Luther's Explanation of the Second Article).

6. What does faith mean in this perspective? Very
simply these things: Faith is reception of the gift of freedom; faith is rejoicing that the good news of what God
has already done has come; faith is coming alive to
Christ's lordship; faith is trusting that this victory is for
me; faith is becoming aware of the consequences of
God's act for me. Salvation does not come into being
at the moment of a man's faith, nor does it in any way
depend upon man's faith, but the gift of salvation becomes real and efficacious for a man through his faith.

In World War II, Norway was occupied by German
forces while the free nations were fighting the Axis
powers on the fields of France. When the Germans sur-
rendered unconditionally Norway was free, although
she had not fought in the war—we can put aside the
underground for purposes of our illustration. The German occupation forces laid down their arms without a
struggle, and the freed Norwegians put them in cus-
tody. But far up north in Lapland the news traveled
slowly. For several weeks the Norwegians there were
free, but they did not know it. Their freedom had been
won, but they did not yet enjoy its benefits.

Three situations can result in a context like this. First,
it is possible to be free but not know it and therefore
not exercise that freedom. Second, it is possible to hear
that freedom has been won but refuse to believe it or
act upon it. Freedom still actually eludes those who are

free. Third, it is possible to hear and to believe and then to experience and possess that freedom. In all three cases, however, there is no doubt as to the reality of the battle and of the freedom. The only doubt is who will hear and who will believe.

There are both strengths and weaknesses in this picture, as there are in all interpretations. We must be rigorously honest in assessing them.

First, the strengths:

1. Salvation is an act of total grace, that is, God's whole work of love. There is no doubt that the V.P. says this more clearly and profoundly than any other view.

2. Evil is presented as the reality that it is—the irrational, objective power that engulfs the human race. Some other views, as we shall see, concentrate on the individual to such an extent that they forget the corporate and cosmic dimensions of God's work.

3. Christ is pictured as exalted Lord, the main New Testament theme, and in a way which fits in directly with the best understanding of the resurrection.

4. The corporateness of man's existence—his involvement with other men and with his own past history—is here preserved in a way that is close to modern man's experience of interdependence and interresponsibility with other men.

Second, the weaknesses:

1. Modern secular man requires such literal, logical

language in order to understand a concept that he may find the highly dramatic and suggestive imagery difficult to apply to himself. This is not a certain weakness, because the V.P. also uses language that is especially meaningful to modern men in other contexts, such as freedom, evil, and battle.

2. The guilt of sin does not receive sufficient emphasis. To be sure, man shares in the responsibility for evil and thus is guilty, and his guilt is forgiven by God as surely as in any other interpretation, but this aspect is not the main thrust. Forgiveness, at least in the Reformation tradition, has carried such a heavy load that any understanding of the faith that does not use it explicitly seems very strange. Many people forget that forgiveness is a broad term embracing the idea of the whole relationship between men and God and does not refer only to forgiveness of specific sins. Luther equated forgiveness with life and salvation. Nevertheless, the question of guilt cannot be slighted in any degree.

3. Because the cosmic significance is so prominent, it is only a small logical jump to the idea of universalism—a word which often, although not always, means that all men will be saved. This need not be the case, however, for although God's love is for all men, it is lost on some when it is not received and the freedom God won, at great sacrifice, is never appropriated. Any picture of God which emphasizes his love will have logical problems as to how far this is to be extended. The V.P. answer is simple: It is for all, but not all re-

ceive. But the problem of universalism persists and its dangers ought to be carefully noted.

We will return to this in our summary.

The Sacrifice

A second picture is directly attributed to Anselm who, as we have noted, started the whole discussion with his little book *Why God Became Man.* Subsequent generations have amplified and modified Anselm's proposal, but the main lines remain. Christ is presented as the sacrifice for man's sin, the substitution for the man who deserved punishment and the satisfaction for the demands of God's law. Various names have become attached to this theory—sacrificial (quite obviously), transaction (forgiveness given in exchange for the satisfaction of God's justice), penal, Latin, and even others. We will refer to it as the Sacrificial Picture (S.P.). It is safe to say that this has been the dominant theme in western Christianity, in both the Roman Catholic and the Lutheran traditions. One reason for this is that Europe and North America are products of the religious and cultural environment of the Middle Ages. Lutherans did not challenge this understanding of the atonement, although Luther also revived the V.P. The Lutheran confessions have leaned toward the S.P. emphasis, and as a result we have very often found these two approaches to the atonement side by side in Lutheranism. Perhaps as often, however, one or the other has dominated.

The diagram is like this:

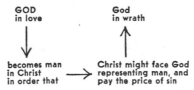

The sequence of events is simple. God, motivated by his love for men, becomes man in order that he may provide the perfect sacrifice for man's sins. Christ takes the place of man before the God of wrath, accepts the punishment, and thus makes it possible for God to be both holy and loving.

Again a time-honored illustration comes to mind. The scene is a courtroom. A judge, loving the law, is forced to pass sentence on a defendant who happens to be his own son. There is no doubt as to the son's guilt, and there is no doubt as to the punishment which the law demands—death. The judge pronounces the correct sentence and then gets off the bench, goes to the prisoner's docket, and takes the place of his condemned son, an act which is permitted in a heavenly courtroom.

Some sentences come to mind here, too:

And the Lord has laid on him the iniquity of us all
(Isa. 53:6).
Who was put to death for our trespasses (Rom. 4:25).
. . . he has appeared once for all at the end of the age to put away sin by the sacrifice of himself (Heb. 9:26).

> There was no other good enough
> To pay the price of sin,
> He only could unlock the gate
> Of heaven, and let us in.
>   (SBH, 77:4)

Another analysis of these elements is necessary.

1. The role of God here is more complicated. God is both the one who is active in providing the sacrifice and the one who receives the sacrifice. God, motivated by love, becomes man in order to become one with man, accepting his guilt. And then as man, Christ faces the God of wrath, who demands recompense. God plays two roles: love, which gives, and holiness, which demands. The problem dealt with in the atonement is God's sense of justice. God wants to love men, but he must channel his love through the demands of the law. God must serve both love and justice. The tension between love and justice becomes a problem solved in full view of the human race. The solution of this problem is what the atonement is.

Christ acts two roles too. He is the one who comes from God and the one who faces God. As the one who is both perfect and the sin-bearer, he represents both God and man. The whole setting is within the context of the relationship between the God of love and the God of wrath (the same God) and between God and guilty man. The world, as evil, is not in the picture as a third element at all.

2. Man is the guilty one. Man has disobeyed God and is judged and condemned for it. If he is not to be lost forever, the guilt must be removed. Man is caught in a legal bind. He must pay the punishment, and yet he cannot, for even infinite punishment, which is not within his power to pay, would not recompense God. So

man's guilt, rather than the power of evil, must be removed, and this is done by involving man indirectly in the atonement itself and, as we shall see, directly in the act of salvation.

3. Evil is understood "existentially," that is, within the life of man, and especially in my life. The emphasis is upon the very personal character of sin, especially seen in its psychological aspects of anxiety, guilt, and release.

4. Salvation is not equated with atonement as in the V.P. The atonement, the placating of God's wrath, prepares the way for salvation, which occurs later when the sinner repents. Atonement is the foundation for salvation and is therefore different and separate from salvation. God, being freed from the demand of his own law, may forgive men without limit. The reconciliation between God and man takes place in the present moment when man repents of his sin and accepts this forgiveness. Atonement is a past, objective event pinpointed in the death of Christ. Salvation is a present event dependent upon the character of man's response. This is not suggesting that man's faith creates salvation, but it does mean that salvation is defined somewhat differently as to its nature.

5. How is atonement accomplished? This is clearly answered within the framework of a legal scheme. Christ pays the punishment for man's sins, satisfying God's justice and permitting God to love without reservation. This is a solution to God's problem which is

ethically responsible. Indeed the whole approach is very cognizant of the demands of right procedure, logical analysis, and a complete solution to man's guilt. Three words are very important: *(a)* sacrifice—God was willing to give himself to help man; *(b)* satisfaction—man need not feel guilty any longer because the holy God is still both holy and forgiving; *(c)* substitution—Christ becomes the Savior because he took my place. My love and gratitude goes to him. Bernard of Clairvaux expresses it:

> What language shall I borrow
> To thank thee, dearest friend,
> For this thy dying sorrow,
> Thy pity without end?
> (SBH, 88:3)

6. What is faith? Faith is believing that God has forgiven me. To recognize sin and accept guilt, to see the sacrifice of Christ to the Father as an expiation (payment) for sin, to receive God's offer of forgiveness for Christ's sake—all this is faith.

What are the strengths and weaknesses here?

First, the strengths:

1. The S.P. deals simply, realistically, and completely with the question of man's guilt and God's justice.

2. Man's problem of guilt, a psychological fact common to the whole human race—sometimes called by other names, such as anxiety or estrangement—is directly solved. And man is seen in his inner self as a person whose problems are mainly individual and spiritual.

3. Western man's assumption that justice is an ideal, that is, an overriding fact of human reality, makes communication of this picture at least apparently possible. It is, to put it bluntly, a civilized approach to religion, psychologically verifiable and philosophically respectable.

And the weaknesses:

1. There is the question as to whether or not the legalistic formulation is the most apt way to see the reconciliation between God and man. Is there the danger that the S.P. deals with an abstract problem of justice and punishment rather than with real personal categories, the real world in which I live, and the real God, the God of love? Has the Old Testament understanding of sacrifice been twisted to fit a humanistic and philosophic idea?

2. If this picture is a bit overdrawn in its logical conclusion, must one not conclude (as Calvin did) that some men *must* be saved and others *must* be damned? This is not a necessary result because pictures of this kind cannot be pushed to their ultimate end, but the danger is there (the V.P. has the opposite danger) and has actually resulted in harsh edicts of predestination.

3. If we are rigorously honest with ourselves, what is the picture of God that lingers after this analysis? The intention is to preach the Gospel of love. Is this what actually happens? Or is it the God of wrath that is more deeply imprinted? You judge.

4. What shall we do with the world itself, with evil as a reality that has corporate dimensions? And what does the resurrection mean here?

The Magnet

The third picture is the simplest of all—and the most inviting and perhaps the most dangerous. One ought always to be a bit wary of any solution to a great problem that is too simple—it is usually very powerful in its simplicity and therefore liable to blind us to any weakness. This picture is usually called the Moral Influence theory, a rather unwieldy name. We choose to call it the Magnet Picture, because Jesus is interpreted as the revelation of the love of God that draws men back to him. This view has been especially popular in our era. Our age has generally wanted to shy away from difficult theological propositions and philosophical formulations. We are an anti-philosophical and an anti-intellectual generation. But in fairness we ought to say that it has been very popular because we live in a time which desperately needs simple and direct love.

The diagram is so simple as to hardly be a diagram at all:

God extends his
love to us in the
suffering Jesus

Men are drawn to God
by this overwhelming love

There is really no sequence of events here. The atonement is the revelation of God's matchless love, which is climaxed in the suffering and death of his Son. When man responds to this love in love, atonement (or at-one-ment) or reconciliation occurs. Which, of course, is true.

Some sentences come to mind:

We love, because he first loved us (1 John 4:19).

. . . and I, when I am lifted up from the earth, will draw all men to myself (John 12:32).

Jesus loves me, this I know,
For the Bible tells me so.

We can use fewer words to analyze this picture.

1. God is the seeking lover, the shepherd hunting for the lost sheep, the father forgiving his wayward son. The problem is neither justice, nor evil, nor guilt, but rather man's darkened mind. God acts to overcome man's blindness by opening a window to heaven so that man may look at God's very heart. Jesus is the victim of man's callousness, but by this very sacrifice of love a power is generated to bring men back to God. Jesus is the magnet, the nearly irresistible force that overcomes all obstacles and reconciles God and man. Jesus is mediator in a very special sense—between God and man, bridging the gap.

2. Man is lost, ignorant, lonely, unhappy. His basic need is for direction, a lamp for his pathway, a belongingness, a helping hand. Men are like children, naughty, perhaps even doing very evil things, but basically re-

sponsive to love properly proffered. God is willing to forgive, but man must be willing to respond

3. Sin is ignorance which results in distrust and disobedience. It is a terrible thing, of course, because it keeps God and man apart, but it is not greater than love, since it has no intrinsic power of its own, and it is dispersed and scattered by love. Love conquers all.

4. Salvation is the reconciliation between God and man. This takes place in the present moment when God's love revealed in Christ becomes real and is accepted by a return of love. Atonement, reconciliation, and salvation are equated, as in the V.P. but occur *now* and are decisively subjective, that is, they occur within the Christian life and experience—as compared to the objective character of the V.P. and the S.P.

This is an entirely personalistic setting. One person hurts another, and this breaks the relationship between them. The relationship is restored only when the guilty one repents and asks forgiveness. The significant aspect is that the guilty party is encouraged to ask for forgiveness by the proffered love of the offended one.

5. How does it happen? Obviously, God came into history in the humble form of a carpenter from Nazareth to show man how deep, profound, and endless is his love for all men. He became a man for others. Men mistreated and misunderstood him and he, true to his nature, accepted death calmly, thereby reinforcing his purpose to display God's love to his dying breath. The

meaning is powerful, complete, and irresistible. How can anyone withstand such love?

> Love so amazing, so divine,
> Demands my life, my soul, my all.
>
> (SBH, 503:4)

The strengths are clear:

1. This view pictures the atoning work of God in such stark and simple terms that even children may believe and .understand

2. Man is addressed directly in categories that are true to his own experience and can even be verified in daily human relationships.

The weaknesses also are clear:

1. The question is clearly raised as to whether or not sin can be described chiefly as ignorance and incapacity. Sin is also this, but has not the whole dreadful cost of the cross been devalued by an understanding of sin which is only this?

2. If the atonement is primarily revelation of truth rather than an action accomplishing something in itself, there is the possibility that faith becomes either a sentiment, and therefore insipid and quite meaningless, or a sophisticated intellectualism, and therefore insipid and meaningless.

What Does This Mean?

In a sense we have been answering this question all along, for these interpretations of the atonement are themselves attempts to communicate meaning. But we need to stop to survey the whole situation. How shall we relate these three interpretations to each other? Each, we said, has a biblical basis and each has been meaningful to a large section of Christendom.

Each speaks in its own voice to my need. The V.P. is probably the most basic picture in my theology at this stage of my understanding of the New Testament. I see the S.P. and the M.P. as further interpretations of the Victory theme. My reasons are:

(a) The picture of the Christ as the Conqueror speaks very powerfully. It touches the particular world that I have experienced. I have fought in a war, I have been interested in social problems, and I am much affected by the peculiar problems of a nuclear age. For me, the Christ who does battle with evil and offers me freedom becomes the magnet who draws me to him.

(b) Further, the V.P. preserves more clearly the dominant New Testament understanding of Jesus as Lord— which we shall discuss in the next chapter in more detail. Christ is the one who unites all things, who rules over all, and who will come again. Part of my prejudice, I realize, is my unashamed preference for the Apostle Paul. The glorious Easter hymn by Edmond Budry expresses this:

> Thine is the glory, Risen, conquering Son;
> Endless is the victory, Thou o'er death hast won.
>
> (SBH, 566:1)

(c) The Lutheran tradition, with its emphasis upon grace, the gift of faith, the objective character of salvation, and the reality of the world around us, is better understood in the context of this imagery.

(d) The life of the church, especially the aspects of preaching and the Sacraments, becomes heightened. Preaching becomes proclamation of the good news rather than persuasion or proof. The Sacraments become celebrations of God's proffered grace, already won, rather than vehicles which create grace. Baptism is being grafted into the kingdom and the cutting off from the world of evil. As stated in the baptismal liturgy:

> Do you renounce the devil, and all his works, and all his ways?   (SBH, p. 243)

The Lord's Supper is a celebration of the real presence of the living and risen Lord, already in the church, and not only a memorial to a past sacrifice (which it also is, of course).

For these reasons, I suggest that the V.P. is especially relevant and meaningful to this generation. Its weaknesses can be overcome or guarded against. A theology using the vocabulary of freedom can and ought to be constructed for the age in which we live. "For freedom Christ has set us free" (Gal. 5:1).

Many Christians will find their emotional home in the S.P. I must confess that I find this understanding close to my heart as well. Certainly the themes of sacrifice and substitution are bedrock New Testament ideas and cannot be dismissed. But I hesitate slightly to give this view equal standing with the V.P.

(a) This picture is too often distorted into an uncritical satisfaction idea, with God presented as an angry judge demanding the full measure of the law. The whole contribution of the Reformation as a reassertion of the grace of God seems to be nullified by this emphasis. Note that I say that this is a distortion—but a common one.

(b) The problems confronting modern man are greater than his own personal guilt. Our age has problems of demonic powers which need attention, and Christ must be interpreted from more than a psychological point of view. There must be a way to relate the Christian Gospel to the real problems men face in the world about them and not only the problems which they find within themselves.

The V.P. and the S.P. correct, supplement, and complement each other. Seen together, they safeguard each other and probe the depths of the atonement.

The M.P. troubles me. Of course, it is true and it is powerful. But if this picture is taken alone, as liberal theology usually took it, the uniqueness of the Christ evaporates. Love is then a nameless power and the common element of every religion, Christian or not. Christianity seen primarily as revelation of truth rather than God's action slips easily into a philosophical religion, torn from history and finally either only emotion or spiritualism.

This wonderful picture should always be used as a method of communicating the truth of the other two approaches. As a preaching tool, it is unmatched. The goal of both the V.P. and the S.P. is to proclaim the grace of God, based upon specific accomplishments by God which affect both man's inner and outer life.

Jesus died for me.

This is the faith.

. . . he descended into hell;
the third day he rose from the dead;
he ascended into heaven,
and sitteth on the right hand of God
the Father almighty . . .

5.
The Right Hand

Back at the beginning we talked a bit about how we were going to treat the subject of the Christ. We said that we intended to talk from the context of commitment and use a language that is concerned with ideas and meanings. Our chief concerns were not analyses of particular biblical texts or historical events. We agreed, however, that one cannot and should not ever escape the historical claims of the New Testament when interpreting the Christ. At the same time we recognized that history and interpretation are intermingled to such an extent that they cannot always be separated cleanly and clearly.

The discussion about the incarnation was rooted in the birth of the baby Jesus, a very real and in a sense ordinary event. A baby was born and we asked the question, What was the significance of that birth? We thought it had a rather important significance! The life of Jesus was an ordinary life in many respects—he ate, slept, argued, walked, etc.—but our interest was not in the ordinariness of that life but in the meaning. The death of Jesus, too, was a real and ordinary death (if one ever dares say that about death) involving the heart, the brain, pain, and eyewitnesses, but we looked at this agony from the point of view of its eternal importance and analyzed pictures of the atonement.

About History and Hell

So far so good. Our discussion has always been within the historical context, that is, we have talked about nature, time and space, and our own existence. We used rather symbolic expressions at times. For example, we spoke of God coming "into" history as though history has an "outside" like a milk carton. We could have talked (although we did not) about his death in terms of "leaving" history, as though we could pop in and out of history as we enter and leave a room. We were willing to live with some of this vagueness simply because we did not have the space to examine it critically and we made the assumption that such language is common enough among Christians so that we could be understood.

But now we have come to the point where we have to pause a moment and ask some searching questions. Suddenly we are asked to deal with some "events" which occurred "after" the death of Jesus. "He descended into hell," says the creed, and "the third day he rose from the dead; he ascended into heaven, and sitteth on the right hand . . . ." Are these events historical? That is, are they the kind of things that we can label as being within the scope of human existence? Do they touch upon nature, time and space, empirical investigation and measurement, and all the rest? We had some problems before in understanding even when we had material that seemed at first glance to be quite ordinary history. What now when we are dealing with ideas that belong to the life of God "outside" of ordinary experience?

Much depends upon the way we use our words. Most of us have been so conditioned by the scientific approach to life that we find it difficult to think in biblical terms. Is history a word, for example, that we should use in talking about the life and existence of God? Many people would say yes. We must treat the resurrection as an event in the same way as other events that can be reported in newspapers, proved by historical investigation, and believed or not believed on the basis of available evidence. They are very anxious, as a result, to examine the historical basis of the resurrection in the New Testament in order to find out what *really* happened. This is an honorable and necessary pursuit, and I shall not challenge it here, except to say that as important as this is, it will not get to the root of the New Testament message. There is something more to be said than can be encompassed in the proof or disproof of a man rising out of a grave. And that is what we are going to try to say.

We choose to speak of God's life as being "outside" our human history. This is another way of saying that God is not subject to the limitations of human existence but has his own existence. God has his own kind of history. The events after Christ's death are God's history happening in such a way that our history is affected. There were witnesses to this resurrection history, too, but the witness is couched in such a way in the New Testament that I, for one, am forced to the conclusion that it is not subject to the scientific approach to the validation of history that we generally accept in other areas of life. If there are any professional philosophers reading this book, they will probably accuse us of going off into a realm of discourse that is no longer intelligible to a modern man. Such a statement is not wholly true. We can say that it is true in the sense that Christian talk about the meaning of Christ after his death belongs to the realm of faith and is not intelligible to someone who chooses to look at life from another perspective.

Are the descent into hell, the resurrection, and the ascension history? The answer—it depends upon how terms are defined. They are not, in any case, ordinary history.

First, we will make a little excursion into the meaning of "he descended into hell." This little phrase has troubled many people and has consequently assumed a place in their thinking far beyond its significance for the faith. Whether or not it was part of the original creed is questionable, and its roots in the New Testament are rather shallow.[1] It certainly did not become common thinking in the church before the fourth century, and most confessions in the Protestant tradition raise more questions about this than they answer. The final answer is left to heaven itself. The Formula of Concord, the most profound and detailed Lutheran confession, which is not known for being bashful about taking explicit positions on controversial matters, exhibits unusual humility of spirit in this case. "How this took place is something that we should postpone until the other world, where there will be revealed to us not only this point, but many others as well . . . ."[2]

Two schools of thought have grown up around this article of faith. The first interprets hell as being hades, that is, the realm of the dead. The phrase means, quite simply, that Jesus descended into death, that is, he really died. Calvin said it most explicitly—Jesus suffered in his soul the dreadful torments of a person who is condemned and lost. The idea is closely related to the dying words of Jesus "My God, my God, why hast thou forsaken me?" (Matt. 27:46). This is a deeply moving and profound interpretation, a significant part of the faith, whether or not it is expressed in these words in the creed. There is no reason why this interpretation could not suffice, since it is true.

Luther was a bit unsure of his own understanding here and gave several interpretations during the course of his career as a teacher. The Formula of Concord suggests, and it is generally accepted by Lutherans, that this phrase points to the victory of Christ over hell and the devil. He descended into hell to announce his victory. It becomes then a symbol for the Victory Picture of the atonement. Christ has redeemed us from the power of death and evil. The *descensus* (as it is technically called) is therefore repeating a view of the atonement and is inserted into the creed to insure that interpretation. This would reflect accurately the thinking of the church in the fourth century—and if you have followed the views of the author, our thinking as well.

Kept within the context of these two interpretations, this phrase assumes a relevant and helpful place in the language of the faith. Some people want (and have) this phrase taken out of the creed because, they say, it only causes confusion. They have every right to think so and to refuse to use it. On the other hand, we have every right to suggest that this ancient and highly symbolic sentence can be properly interpreted and thus add meaning to the faith—as it no doubt will for most of Christendom.

The Resurrection

We said, rather rashly perhaps, that the chapter on the atonement was the most important part of the book. We meant it, but now we are going to say that the resurrection is just as important. We can do so with some consistency because the resurrection and the atonement go together. They are inseparable. They are not two events which can be treated without reference to each other. We discuss them in two different chapters only because it seemed logical to progress from one thought to another and not talk about everything at once.

What do we mean by this?

Back on page 7 we suggested some homework. Get it out now and compare with the following. You most likely discovered that the accounts of the resurrection present us with a series of very difficult textual problems. They fall into three classes:

1. There are some seeming contradictions. No two of the Gospels, for example, have the same women coming to the tomb on Easter morning. Mark has Mary Magdalene, Mary the mother of James, and Salome (Mark 16:1). The two Marys and Joanna are in Luke's account (24:10). Matthew mentions only the two Marys (28:1). Mark has the women come to the tomb very early in the morning but after the sun had risen (16:2). John, however, says that Mary Magdalene came when it was still dark (20:1) and Matthew says simply "toward the dawn" (28:1). The identity of the messenger at the tomb is recorded variously. Mark has a young man clothed in a long white garment (16: 5, 6), Luke two men in shining garments (24:4-6), Matthew an angel of the Lord (28:2-5), and John two angels (20:12, 13). In Mark (16:4) and Luke (24:2) the women find the stone rolled away, but in Matthew the stone is miraculously rolled away by an angel, and he adds the story of the

earthquake which accompanied it. Only Matthew has the story of the sealing of the tomb and the mounting of a guard (27:62-66).

2. A second problem, perhaps not noticed by the casual reader, is the place of the appearances of Jesus. Mark ends at Mark 16:8, as most new translations show. Mark 16:9-20 is a later addition. The resurrection is recorded in Mark 16:1-8, but no appearances are related and no place at all is therefore recorded.

In Matthew there is the appearance to the women on their way back to Jerusalem from the tomb (28:9 f.) but this is brief and fleeting. The important appearance for Matthew is the one in Galilee (28:16-20), which is to the disciples. In Luke all the appearances are in the vicinity of or in Jerusalem (24:13-53). Luke further complicates his story by making it appear that the ascension takes place on the same day as the resurrection (24:50-51). The New English Bible does not put the phrase "and was carried up into heaven" into the text but in a footnote. The early writer who added this phrase was unaware of or unconcerned about the appearance recorded in Matthew.

John has a resurrection appearance to Mary in the garden and to the disciples in Jerusalem in John 20, but suddenly in John 21 the scene shifts to the disciples by the lakeside in Galilee.

Questions arise because (a) Jesus had predicted in Mark 14:28 that he would meet his disciples in Galilee (which they evidently did not take seriously), not in

Jerusalem and *(b)* because the Gospel writers do not
seem to be aware (or at least are not paying much attention) that something strange is going on in their tell-
ing of the appearances in two places without any con-
nection.

3. The third puzzle is the question of the empty
tomb. Although Paul asserts the facticity of the resurrection event in 1 Corinthians 15 in no uncertain terms,
he does not base it on the evidence of the empty tomb.
Peter does not mention it in his great sermon in Acts 2,
although the whole sermon is intoxicated with the idea
of the resurrection. In fact, those who talk the most
about the resurrection do not mention the empty tomb.
What are we to make of this?

We have not assumed the burden of solving the historical riddles in the New Testament, but something
needs to be said about this because it troubles so many
people. Two matters are important: First, the discrep-
ancies, many of which are trifling, only serve to verify
the essential historical flavor of the stories. People involved in such profoundly emotional experiences do
not remember details well. We might have suspected
the stories if they had been perfectly consistent and
correct in every detail. Second, it is very important to
note that the New Testament writers are not especially
concerned about these details. They chose not to
achieve perfect agreement in their reporting, and this
in itself may tell us something significant. The historical
details of the resurrection, although inescapably there,

are not the main concern and therefore not the main message of the biblical writer.

There is something more.

1. The appearances of the risen Christ inspired worship. We have previously called attention to the climax of the Gospel of John in the cry of Thomas, "My Lord and my God!" This worship response occurred every time he came; he carried an aura of glory with him. This was not the Jesus they had been with before *exactly*. It was and it was not. Now he was to be worshiped without question; before they had wondered and quarreled about him.

2. Another curious feature is that some of the time they did not recognize him. The two travelers on the way to Emmaus did not (Luke 24:16), Mary Magdalene did not (John 20:14), and the disciples by the lakeside were rather unsure (John 21:4, 12). Jesus was there, *in his body,* and yet there was something decidedly different about him.

3. The appearances are described as being extraordinary in other ways. Jesus comes and goes without any reference to distance, space, or time. He vanishes from sight (Luke 24:31), he walks through closed doors (John 20:19, 26), and he looks like a spirit (Luke 24:37), but he eats, unlike a spirit (Luke 24:39-43). Mary Magdalene is forbidden to touch him (John 20:17), but Thomas is asked to do so (John 20:27). The aspects of our history do not seem to apply to him precisely.

4. Paul applied his great intellect to this whole matter and had great difficulty in finding words to convey meaning. He struggles to find some way of talking about the nature of Jesus after the resurrection and he finally hits upon the strange (for a Jew) phrase "spiritual body" (1 Cor. 15:44).

It is time to draw some conclusions.

1. The resurrection of Jesus is incomprehensible. The New Testament says, very clearly, that it is dealing with an event which simply does not fit into the ordinary categories of either language or human experience. It is something which is related to history, for it was intimately involved with the lives of people, but it was involved in such a way as to defy description in terms of ordinary human existence. And the New Testament seems to be saying that any attempt to make of this a neat, consistent, logical, and empirically verifiable event is to destroy it.

We have to live by faith, after all.

Let us try another diagram:

The line here represents the division between the earthly life of Jesus, which we called the state of humiliation, and his resurrected life, which we called exaltation—a line which *is* the events of his death and resurrection. The one side of the line is historical time and the other is God's time, eternity. One of the helpful ways to approach the complexities of the resurrection is to analyze the relationship between these two states of being. In what ways is the Jesus who was in history different from and/or similar to the resurrected Lord of all?

The following ideas are involved:

(a) There is continuity, that is, the Jesus who rose from the dead did so at a time that follows, chronologically, the time of his death. There is a sequence of events that shows all the characteristics of ordinary history. First he dies and then he is raised from the dead.

(b) This sequence, furthermore, is irreversible. He does not rise continually, as in the pagan myths, but once, uniquely. His death was real, and his resurrection was real in the sense that this is not a parable that can be told without relation to something that happened and cannot happen again.

(c) There is something we can call identity. The Jesus who rose from the dead is the same one who died. This is very important to say, as elementary as it sounds. Jesus of Nazareth was not laid to rest only to have a ghost of some kind rise over his body to become his continuing spirit. No, the same Jesus who walked the dusty roads of Galilee also walked to Emmaus.

(d) But there is also a radical discontinuity. Although it was the identical Jesus who rose from the dead, it was Jesus in a different state and form. Perhaps those are wrong words but better ones have not come along. Before he was the humiliated one; now he is the exalted one. Before he was limited to time and space; now he is the Lord of time and space. He is the same, and yet he is different. He is not like Lazarus, who after his resurrection was the same Lazarus as before, subject again to death. Jesus is raised forever!

2. The resurrection has several dimensions of meaning:

(a) It is a historical event. It happened one day. We say this with confidence even though there were no witnesses to the resurrection itself. There were witnesses only to the appearances. Yet the New Testament speaks in such a way that to draw the conclusion, as some have done, that this is only a subjective event in the minds of the disciples is to do violence to the clear intention. The New Testament writers may have been misled, but we do not believe this. From faith to faith!

(b) It is *also* a "non-historical" event. We may be doing violence to words by saying this, but some violence is necessary. This event does not fit into ordinary experience. It has a reality all its own. It is utterly unique.

(c) We must also accept the dimension of subjectivity. The resurrection understood *only* as an objective

historical event is rather meaningless—that is, it does not accomplish its purpose simply through acknowledgment of its factualness. The reaction of the disciples in faith is an important element. The joy, the assurance, the hope, the enthusiasm, indeed the new life itself (resurrection *is* the new life in John's Gospel) are part of the resurrection event. Christ is risen for those who accept him in faith.

(d) This leads us to say that the resurrection also has a corporate character. The resurrection belongs to the church, the community of faith. Jesus always appeared to the group, or to someone who was related to a group—"Go tell the disciples." The resurrection is the event which creates the Christian church, and its power is within the border of the people of God.

3. The resurrection is, with the atonement, the center of the message of Christianity. Acts, which is the story of the earliest church, and therefore an index to early thinking, has been correctly called the Gospel of the resurrection. There is not a sermon in it in which the resurrection is not the central theme—Acts 2:24, 32; 3:15, 26; 4:10, 33; 5:30; 10:40; 13:30-34; 17:31. Paul's First Letter to the Corinthians, which was most likely written before the earliest of the Gospels, commits itself to the resurrection in irrevocable terms (1 Cor. 15).

4. The resurrection is an act of God and thus part of his work of redemption. The verb used consistently in the New Testament about the resurrection is in the pas-

sive voice. He *has been* raised would be the more precise translation. Jesus was raised by God. He did not rise from the grave because of an innate power of immortality, or as an act of his own will, or because of some inevitable necessity, but because God acted to raise him. Seen from the perspective in which God has placed us, the resurrection assumes its proper place with the virgin birth, the miracles, and the death as events *through* which God has acted to redeem us. The resurrection is not an afterthought but an essential part of the whole.

The Ascension

The ascension is described most fully in Acts 1:1-12 and is mentioned briefly in Mark 16:19 and Luke 24:51, and perhaps also in John 20:17, 27. Many other references refer to Jesus being at the right hand of God, that is to say, returned to the Father and in a state of exaltation. There is massive evidence that the New Testament accepts the ascension as an integral part of the faith.

We want to emphasize three points:

1. One interesting aspect, from the historical point of view, is the question of the 40 days. We celebrate the ascension on the sixth Thursday after Easter, taking our cue from Acts. It must be remembered, however, that in Hebrew thought, 40 days is not necessarily an arithmetic idea but rather describes an indefinite length of time. Forty days is used of the flood (Gen. 7:12, 17),

of the stay of Moses on Mount Sinai (Ex. 24:18), and of the time of the temptation of Jesus (Matt. 4:2). Exact measurement of time is not in the mind of the writers. And neither is space. The picture of the ascension that should come to mind is not that of an Atlas rocket streaking into the sky to a rendezvous at a point in space called the right hand of God. Space considerations do not really apply. Jesus ascended into a cloud, that is, into the presence of God.

2. It is necessary, nevertheless, to apply one important time idea. The ascension is the noting of the end of the involvement of God in history in this way. The ascension is the terminating event. This act is over. The next act of the play begins. We are not to stand gazing into heaven. Jesus will not appear to us as he did to the disciples. He has chosen to go away, that is, to change the form by which he works with us. The Apostolic Age is over. That age was unique. We live in the age of the church and the Holy Spirit (a subject for still another book).

3. But most important of all is the witness of the ascension to Christ's exaltation. He is Lord. And this brings us to our summary.

What Does This Mean?

The meaning is stark, uncompromising, all-encompassing.

Jesus Christ is Lord. He is my Lord. He is our Lord. He is the Lord of all.

There are many titles for the Christ in the New Testament, and we, regretfully, have had to pass by the fascinating task of analyzing them. At this point we can only say that all the titles converge in the one supreme title Lord.

The title Lord grows, in the development of the reflection of the church, from a common title of respect, very close to Sir or Mister in English, to the equivalent of God. This growth can be demonstrated by an analysis of the more than 600 usages in the New Testament, a formidable study in itself. The climactic usage, as the divine name, is used at least 150 times in the New Testament.

Three dimensions of meaning must be noted:

1. Jesus Christ is the ultimate reality for me. When I call him Lord I attribute to him absolute mastery over my life, my possessions, my hopes, my fears. He is my God. He is a present living reality. I pray to him, give him my adoration and praise, and center my understanding of myself and the world in him.

2. Further, he is our Lord. That is, he is the head, the ruler of the church. He dwells in his church, energizes it, feeds it, comforts it, and leads it. This is what we mean by his presence in the Sacraments and the ministry of the Word (remember what this means) of God.

3. But there is still more. He is at the right hand of God, that is, he is the Ruler of the whole universe. He is the agent through whom God exercises his dominion

over all of history and nature. He is Lord of lords. He is the regulatory principle of all that is.

In this role he is also judge—and there is the excuse to begin another chapter.

Footnotes

[1]Matthew 27:52 f.; Romans 10:6, 7; Ephesians 4:8-10; 1 Peter 3:18-20.

[2]Article XI, "Christ's Descent into Hell" The Formula of Concord in *The Book of Concord,* translated and edited by Theodore G. Tappert (Philadelphia: Muhlenberg Press, 1959), p. 492.

*. . . from thence he shall come
to judge the quick
and the dead.*

6.

The Mystery of the End

Jesus said he was coming again
We believe him.

But we may not be exactly sure that we understand
fully what he meant. Perhaps we are saying only that
we trust him to do whatever it is he meant. He has not
come yet, we assume. But there is something a bit puz-
zling about this. We have already learned that the
ordinary aspects of history do not seem to apply to biblical words and even events.

There seems to be mystery here, too. It is not too
late to go back to some fundamentals. In Christianity
we seem to go back to fundamentals again and again.
Exactly, for that is what the faith is all about—the fundamentals and the ultimates of our existence.

For example, time.

Time and Time and Time

Imagine that you are on a New York subway. For some of you (who do it every day) that may not be an altogether pleasant idea, but come along, it is useful for our illustrative purposes.

If you stand at the back of the train while it is hurtling through the dark tunnel, you will see only the shadows swallowing up the track you have just passed. In the front of the train you may see a green or red light glowing in the distance, but again everything else is hid from you. You move constantly—the past recedes into oblivion and the future has not yet arrived. In a certain sense, it is only the present which is real. It is only the lighted subway car in which you are that is your existence. Augustine, in one of his more psychological moments, said that the past was really only memory and the future only hope. Time *has* this quality of movement, irreversibility (you are not the driver, you cannot go back, but only forward), and limitation to the present. Indeed the passenger is really a slave to his situation. He cannot reach out and touch the past—it is always retreating. He must wait for the future to arrive. Only an occasional warning or bit of hope lights it up for him.

This is the way the New Testament talks of one kind of time called *chronos* (without the subway, of course). We have already mentioned how important this time is. The movement of time, in the biblical understanding, is not circular, that is, endless repetition, but a straight line—like a subway line. Progress is possible.

Suddenly you come to a station. The train stops for a moment. The station is all lighted up. It extends for some distance forward and some distance behind—if you are in the center car. It is as though the whole world, and it *is* the world of the subway car, were suddenly expanded. The future and the past become more real. You are not conscious of constant movement. The pinpointing of the present moment is blurred and your experience expands. There is added importance and meaning now. Some kind of destination has been reached, some kind of event which is different from the simple movement in the dark tunnel. Some excitement, new horizons, some enlightenment come into play.

This is somewhat the meaning of time which the New Testament calls *kairos*. There is a kind of time which assumes special significance and has content and meaning which is not encompassed in the simple passing from the past into the future. This is a "full" or "ripe" time. It is a simple fact in your own experience that certain moments of time are more important than others—your marriage, a play you saw, an insight that seemed to come from nowhere, an important decision you made, a sorrow—and these moments overshadow all the other moments and are very real to you, whether they happened yesterday or twenty years ago. Indeed your life is really made up of these moments. They are the "times" which give substance and content to life.

When Jesus came to Galilee, preaching and opening his public ministry, he said "The time is fulfilled, and

the kingdom of God is at hand . . ." (Mark 1:15). This
was *kairos* time, a time of great significance. Which year
or day it was, was not really important—indeed is not
even mentioned. Time is measured by what happens in
it, rather than by its quantity. How long Jesus lived is
of little consequence (we do not even know, for that
matter), but what he accomplished is of eternal importance. How long you live is not the most essential element about your life either. But what is dreadfully important is what happened to you while you did live.
A hundred years of meaningless routine cannot compare with twenty years of joy and service.

The time of Jesus was so significant that it engulfs all
of history. Even though it was contained in a few years
of chronological time, and this is very important to remember, the content of that life was such that everything is affected. It is as though his life were the Times
Square subway station, to which all trains come and
from which all trains leave. He is the beginning and the
end, the terminus, the goal of all times. This may be a
supercilious illustration, but maybe a subway for our
time is as meaningful an illustration as the fig tree in the
New Testament!

We are not finished yet. When you reach your destination and get off the train, you ascend to the day-
light world above the ground. Here suddenly there is
again another dimension. In fact, you can look back to
the place where you have just been traveling. What you
could not see in the tunnel as the place of your depar-
ture you can see clearly now. And you can even see be-

yond the spot at which you have arrived. The right and the left can even be seen at one time. Nor do you have to travel to the Statue of Liberty in order to know it. You can sight it from the Empire State Building, before you arrive there by ferry. The Statue would be *here* and *there* at the same time!

In a very limping way, this is an illustration of the way the New Testament thinks about eternity. Eternity may be spoken of as an infinite length of subway line, using chronological time as the standard of measurement. But even this infinite quantity carries with it a sense of overallness and *quality*. Eternity may also be thought of as *continuous present moment,* a sort of all-including *kairos*. This *kairos* would gather in all that is past and future. Eternity would *not* be the absence of time or timelessness, but "full" time—a time of infinite *quality*.

Eternity is God's time. And this is the time of our Lord who is seated at the right hand.

If we are going to explore the mystery of his coming again, we must be aware of all three dimensions of time. If we limit ourselves to the *chronos* time, as we scientifically minded people are inclined to do, we miss the richness of this Gospel and perhaps get ourselves entangled in strange and unnecessary problems.

The Now and the Not Yet

When we think of the second coming, we most often think of some future "end." We should not limit our

thinking to this, however. The Apostles' Creed and the
New Testament do not say "second coming" as though
he will come only twice—once at his incarnation and
once again in some future event. Rather, the Christ not
only came once, in a special way, but he comes again,
and again, and again. He comes in the preaching of the
Word, in the Sacraments, and in our prayer. He has not
removed himself from his creation. With this discussion we are brought to the doctrine of the Holy Spirit,
which we cannot stop to describe, but the point is necessary to make. His presence and his judgment are constant. We are responsible to him each day, not only in
some future day. He is a *present* living reality, remember?

Our job here, however, is to talk about that "end."
The word end can and does have two meanings. End
can mean goal or purpose. The purpose of this book is
to help you understand the Christ. It may not accomplish that purpose even if you come to the end of the
book, that is, finish reading it. On the other hand, there
is the slight chance that this book will already have accomplished its end—opened up new areas of thought
for you—even if you do not ever finish reading it.

A second meaning of end is consummation. That is,
end can mean the chronological end, the last moment,
which can be a climactic conclusion or just the last
item. You can count your dollars for example, and discover that at the end (of your counting) you have
$39.33. That would be a mathematical end but rather
anticlimactic. But to stress the point, someone might

never reach an end, that is, never count the last dollar, and yet be a millionaire. He will have known this somewhere along the way without finishing the job.

We want to look at both senses of this word.

1. Is there a sense in which we can say that God through Christ has already accomplished his purpose and thus has already come? Yes, I think that there is. Jesus speaks in the past tense of the coming of the kingdom. The kingdom came with him. He is the *kairos* and thus also the end. God did whatever he intends to do for men in the event of Christ. There is no other Gospel, no other event, no additional information. This is sufficient, absolute, final. The Gospel is God's only gift. Look for nothing else.

There is a profound truth in this. More technically it is called "realized eschatology." God's purpose, his *eschaton,* is already realized in Christ. All eyes are to be front and center—on Jesus Christ.

We can shift attention to another focal point. If the purpose of God's work is to be the response of the believer, that is, his salvation, it is possible to speak of the end of God's work as the decision for faith. This would change the time element from the past, the Christ event, to the present moment in my life. God accomplishes his purpose *now* in what I am doing. The *eschaton,* the end, is present, occurring now, in the continual coming of our Lord into the lives of this generation. And, of course, it continues to occur in each succeeding generation. This kind of emphasis is some-

times called "existential eschatology" because the coming of Christ is seen through this aspect of God's work
in the existence of the individual and his faith.

The importance of this cannot be denied. Of course,
Christ comes now and, of course, Christ came before.
However, to stop there, as some are inclined to do,
neglects the important dimension of the future.

2. What meaning for the future is there? There are
four things to consider:

(a) Since we are men and not God, the future must
remain for us a mystery. We are on the subway train.
We have not yet arrived at the destination. We shall
experience great moments of comfort, insight, and
hope, but we cannot get off the train. The future has
an openness to us. Trusting in God, we are sure that
the final consummation is in his hands. Confidence in
the future, without knowing exactly what it contains, is
possible. To know that Jesus Christ is Lord already tells
us much about this assurance.

The shape of the mystery, therefore, has been revealed to us. We are not men without hope but men
whose hope is such that we live by faith and not by
sight. This faith is not blind, moreover, but is guided
by certain signs of both danger and joy.

(b) We know that we shall die. Indeed, the most certain thing about our life is our death. Our death will be
an *eschaton,* a fulfillment, in the future. God will consummate his purposes, and one phase of our existence
will come to a final end at a particular moment. Our

destination in this sense is well known to us. It probably is involved in either our unconscious or conscious thinking every waking moment.

God will call us at death and give us new life. Just as he raised Jesus from the dead, so he will raise us up. Then he will judge us. This will not be a new judgment, for we will have been judged all along. Nor will it be a surprising judgment for those who have loved him, for the promise of the Gospel has already told us of the meaning of that reception.

There are some Christians who are anxious to think of death and final judgment only in terms of *chronos* time. We die now but exist through an intermediate state until some future time when, together with the consummate end of all things, the whole human race is judged together.

It is difficult for me to limit myself to this one dimension of time. The many questions that we have about *how* God will raise us have not been answered. If we have rightly ascertained, even to the slightest degree, the possibilities of God's time, of eternity, then the ways of his managing our individual death and his plan for the whole of history are manifold. The possibility of the convergence of some end time and my death in God's life, if not a clear conclusion of the New Testament, is at least as discernible as the more blunt reduction of all future to a *chronos* scheme.

But it is clear to all that death is in our future and that God will use this for his purposes.

(c) With the richness of the concept of time given in

the New Testament, the future becomes more than that for which we wait and prepare. Because of the promises of the Gospel we can enjoy the benefits of that which is not yet *now*. To know our destination is of tremendous comfort even though we have not yet arrived. It shapes our attitudes, governs our decisions, and, in fact, becomes a present reality. The Lord's Supper, for example, is a celebration of God's presence with us now, a presence which will not be more real at some future time but only fuller and perhaps of a different kind. In any case, we, in our anticipation, enjoy his fellowship now.

To say this involves us in some problems. We have already said that the Victory theme is a basic one. Where is the victory? Sin and evil abound around us. Where is the evidence of the redemption now? We must tread carefully in saying that this victory, which was really won in the past and which still has a future dimension, is nevertheless a reality now. We share in the victory won for us. Christ gives us real freedom, but it is a freedom within the framework of a world not yet reconciled to the gift. We live in Lapland. We are still on the subway between Brooklyn and Manhattan island and have a limited insight into what the world above us, under the sun, is like. The little stations along the way give us some insight into the limitless horizons. They are victories of sufficient power to make life itself victorious. In this sense we share in something which we do not yet fully possess.

Seen from the perspective of the dimensions of time,

one could speculate (and it is really only that) that God's time is of such a kind that he can give us the experience of that which has not yet happened. The future, this would say, is in some sense occurring in the midst of our present living. I say speculate because, as enticing as this idea is, its implications are so great and its dimensions so immense that we must shrink back a bit before claiming to have penetrated the mind of God.

There must always be this quality of tension, hope and reflection, daring and humility, when one peers into the future.

(d) The future also, in its mystery, holds that event called the consummation. God will act again, not to add to his Gospel, but to complete it. He will yet bring all things together in a way quite beyond our ability to speak very intelligibly about it. There are some Christians who think that they have had a special insight into this event. I find myself continually surprised and chagrined still to find sincere Christians with maps and charts, proofs and revelations about what God will do— precisely. Indeed, whole denominations have been founded on details of these elaborate forecasts. Their claim is, simply, that they know more about the future than our Lord himself in the flesh claimed to know.

There is a basic misunderstanding here about the nature of some of the language the Bible uses—we keep coming back to the question of language, do we not? Scattered through both the Old and the New Testaments is a way of speaking called apocalyptic language. The Book of Daniel and Revelation abound in it, but we can find it in the Gospels, too, as in Matthew 24, and Luke 21. This is an ecstatic way of communication which has a mixture of poetry, lurid imagery, real history, and what appears to be prediction. It is difficult for us to know, in every instance, precisely what it means. The Book of Revelation, for example, defies clear interpretation. Much is clear but much remains beyond a final and authoritative understanding.

This kind of language seeks to think about the future as though it were already upon us. It speaks about what may belong in the future (or may not) as though it were immediately at hand. Lacking the tools to communicate the message, the writer resorts to this special style. Apocalyptic language is meant both to reveal and to conceal. When it is taken literally, without noting its unique character, much misunderstanding results and the real message may be lost altogether. Once again the conditioning of our era may betray us.

What apocalyptic language tells us: *(a)* There is too much mystery about the future to speak about it in the same way as the present and the past; *(b)* God controls the whole future absolutely and is acting in the present time to bring history to a point of his own choosing; *(c)* God's call to us is urgent and this urgency can be expressed by making the end of his work seem present and pressing; (d) We are to be ready, patient, waiting, trusting; (e) The future does offer hope, for it contains God's final gift.

Very much more cannot be said in this little excursion into a difficult subject.

The Christian life is one which is lived both in the now and the not yet. We live between the times—after the advent, the coming of our Lord in his humiliation, and before the advent of our Lord coming in his glory. It is the first coming that gave us the Gospel and the guidelines for life in the in-between time. The Gospel is itself the promise for the future.

God does not promise a paradise here on earth—indeed, he indicates that evil shall continue, even accelerate. But the ultimate end is clear, for God shall triumph as he has shown us in the victory of the resurrection. We are engaged in a war whose outcome is already determined and whose decisive battle has already been fought and won.

All three dimensions of time—*chronos, kairos,* and eternity—are involved in determining an attitude towards the future. If we limit ourselves to any one, some of the richness disappears and certain dangers of misinterpretation appear.

He came. He continues to come. He is coming.

Indeed, this is the last word of the New Testament—which you ought to look up for yourself in Revelation 22:20.

The Reward

This book has discussed ideas about the Christ. Not every idea has been considered (" . . . were every one of them to be written, I suppose that the world itself could not contain the books . . . " John 21:25), and not every question that has been raised has been adequately answered. Sometimes this was so because the author did not know the answer. At other times it was thought best to leave some room for you, the reader, to do some additional thinking and reading. It may be that there are answers to some of these questions, but they lie in that aspect of the revelation not yet part of the understanding of either you or me.

Writing this little book has been immensely rewarding for me. I would be further rewarded if: *(a)* you filled out the coupon on page 115 and mailed it in; *(b)* you took a serious look at the Bibliography on page 113 and decided to read one or two or more books about the Christ.

You will be rewarded by doing further reading—in this and other subjects. Intellectual growth in the Christian life is as important as any other aspect. Life is too short to come to a full maturity in the ideas God has given us about himself, but the life dedicated to perusal, stimulation, and growth in these ideas will be its own reward.

The chief reward, however, does not lie in the mind. Christianity is not basically a religion of ideas but of deeds. The truth is to be *done*. Actions flow from beliefs, but it is the actions or the life of discipleship which is the gift God aims to give. This is self-evident to those of the faith. It is also a *necessary* response, for it is only in a life lived for others and for the God revealed in Jesus of Nazareth that all of these ideas will begin to have any significant meaning. They will lie inert on these dusty pages until they find expression in daily acts and thoughts.

But when they are put into the ordinary actions of life in the twentieth century, then the one who is Lord of all will become your Lord also, to his everlasting glory and to your eternal salvation.

Bibliography

1. Gustaf Aulén, *Christus Victor* (London: SPCK, 1950). Paperback.

   A short and very well known historical study for those who like to work and think hard

2. William Barclay, *Crucified and Crowned* (London: SCM Press Ltd., 1961). Paperback.

   A Biblical study. Clear, interesting, recommended

3. Robert Clyde Johnson, *The Meaning of Christ* (Philadelphia: The Westminster Press, 1958). Paperback.

   A doctrinal study. Solid, delightful.

4. Reginald H. Fuller, *The New Testament in Current Study* (New York: Charles Scribner's Sons, 1962).

   Also short, for a hard cover book. Concise, a bit technical. For those who want to explore critical problems.

5. Erik Routley, *The Man for Others* (New York: Oxford University Press, 1964). Paperback.

   Inspired by *Honest to God,* a controversial book. This one is not as far out but is challenging to the traditionalist.

6. John S. Whale, *Victor and Victim* (Cambridge: University Press, 1960).

   Intriguing, marvelous. Read it.

Enough for now. One book leads to another.

Tear out and mail

_____
Date

The Book Editor
Augsburg Publishing House
422 South Fifth St.
Minneapolis, Minnesota 55415

Dear Sir:

I have read *His Only Son, Our Lord* and found it:

_____ Dull   _____ Helpful

_____ Interesting   _____ Disturbing

_____ Too easy   _____ You name it

_____ Too difficult

I wish that it would have discussed this topic:

I found this part particularly interesting:

I thought it was wrong on this idea:

My occupation is:

Sincerely,

_____
Name

_____
Address

_____

You may choose to be anonymous.

THE AUTHOR

Kent S. Knutson is professor of systematic theology and director of graduate studies at Luther Theological Seminary, St. Paul, Minn. He came to his present position in 1958 after two years in the U.S. Navy and four years as a pastor in Staten Island, N.Y. He is editor of *Dialog*, a journal of theology, and has contributed chapters to *The New Community in Christ* and *The Silent Struggle for Mid-America*.

Dr. Knutson has a bachelor of science (chemical engineering) degree from Iowa State University, Ames, Iowa, a bachelor of theology degree from Luther Theological Seminary, St. Paul, Minn., and a doctor of philosophy degree from Columbia University, New York. He has done additional study at Heidelberg University and the universities of Oslo and Minnesota.

DATE DUE

APR 1 5 '73			
APR 1 5 '74			
MAY 1 '74			
MAY 1 '75			
MAY 1 5 '79			
MAY 1 5 '80			
APR 2 7 '92			

GAYLORD   PRINTED IN U.S.A.